SCOTTISH SET TEXT GUIDE

National 5 and Higher English

The Cone-Gatherers

Donna Gray

Series Editor:
Carolyn Cunningham

HODDER
GIBSON
AN HACHETTE UK COMPANY

The Publishers would like to thank the following for permission to reproduce copyright material.

Photo credits

p. 10 Carlos G Lopez/Shutterstock; **p. 31** 1tomm/Adobe Stock; **p. 38** alimarc/Adobe Stock; **p. 52** Kay/Adobe Stock; **p.63** pinglabel/Adobe Stock

Acknowledgements

Every effort has been made to trace all copyright holders, but if any have been inadvertently overlooked, the Publishers will be pleased to make the necessary arrangements at the first opportunity.

Although every effort has been made to ensure that website addresses are correct at time of going to press, Hodder Gibson cannot be held responsible for the content of any website mentioned in this book. It is sometimes possible to find a relocated web page by typing in the address of the home page for a website in the URL window of your browser.

Hachette UK's policy is to use papers that are natural, renewable and recyclable products and made from wood grown in well-managed forests and other controlled sources. The logging and manufacturing processes are expected to conform to the environmental regulations of the country of origin.

Orders: please contact Bookpoint Ltd, 130 Park Drive, Milton Park, Abingdon, Oxon OX14 4SE. Telephone: (44) 01235 827827. Fax: (44) 01235 400401. Email education@bookpoint.co.uk. Lines are open from 9 a.m. to 5 p.m., Monday to Friday, with a 24-hour message answering service. Visit our website at www.hoddereducation.co.uk. If you have queries or questions that aren't about an order, you can contact us at hoddergibson@hodder.co.uk

© Donna Gray 2020

First published in 2020 by

Hodder Gibson, an imprint of Hodder Education
An Hachette UK Company
211 St Vincent Street
Glasgow, G2 5QY

Impression number	5	4	3	2	1
Year	2024	2023	2022	2021	2020

Cover photo © imageBROKER/Adobe Stock

Typeset by Integra Software Services Pvt. Ltd., Pondicherry, India

Printed in Italy

A catalogue record for this title is available from the British Library.

ISBN: 978 1 5104 6817 7

Contents

This guide is designed to help you work towards getting the best possible grade in your English examination. It contains a wealth of useful information, not only on the novel *The Cone-Gatherers* itself but also on improving your exam techniques. Using this guide to accompany your study of the novel will help you to greater success in your English examination.

This guide uses the Canongate 2012 edition of *The Cone-Gatherers* by Robin Jenkins, ISBN: 978-0-85786-235-8. All page numbers align with this edition.

It is important that you use this guide throughout your reading and revision – in fact, Chapter 2: Context will help you get to grips with the novel before you even begin to read it.

As you read the novel, referring to Chapter 3: Study and revision will enhance your understanding of literary features such as plot, structure, characterisation, theme and language.

When you have finished reading the novel, the guidance and advice given in Chapter 4: Approaching the Critical Reading paper will support your revision as well as strengthening your understanding of the text. You may be aware that *The Cone-Gatherers* is one of the 'crossover' texts in the English Critical Reading paper: this means that it is an option in National 5 *and* Higher Scottish text sections of the examination paper. Candidates at both levels may decide to use this novel in their responses to the critical essay section of the examination paper. This section of the guide is helpfully divided into National 5 and Higher pages, giving detailed advice on how to deal with the Scottish text and critical essay sections for each level.

The following features have been used throughout this guide to help you gain the most from your study of the novel:

Glossary

This feature highlights and defines key words used in the novel and in this guide.

Target your thinking

You will see this feature at the start of every chapter or main section. It contains questions that provide a focus for what you will learn in that chapter.

Key quotation

This feature will draw your attention to quotations that are important in conveying key aspects of the text.

Exam tip

Top tips to help you maximise your chances of success in the exam.

Build critical skills

This feature appears throughout the guide. It will help you to analyse and explore aspects of the novel in greater depth.

REVIEW YOUR LEARNING

You will see this feature at the end of each chapter. It contains questions that will help you to firm up your knowledge of the novel and/or your understanding of exam techniques.

Preparing to study *The Cone-Gatherers*

There are many different ways of studying the novel and each individual will have a preferred way of approaching a piece of literature. Some will read the text in its entirety before attempting to reflect on its themes, characters and all of the aspects that make it a piece of memorable literature. Others will work through the novel chapter by chapter in the classroom, making notes and discussing particular aspects of the text. Whatever way you read and study the novel, it is important to remember one thing: you must gain an in-depth knowledge and understanding of the text and develop your analytical skills in order to do well in the examination.

Using this guide as a companion to your study of *The Cone-Gatherers* will undoubtedly help you to acquire the depth of knowledge and understanding needed to successfully answer the Scottish text questions and write effective critical essays. It is also worth remembering that basic study techniques – such as highlighting, making notes, creating mind-maps, etc. – are useful in reinforcing your knowledge of a text. It goes without saying that this guide is meant to support your reading of the novel, not replace it. It is important to develop your own thoughts and feelings about the novel as you read it, rather than just memorising the information given in this guide.

The world in which *The Cone-Gatherers* is set is very different from that of the present day. The novel is a work of fiction with characters and events generated in the imagination of its author, Robin Jenkins. The novel draws upon various influences in Jenkins' life – in particular his experiences as a conscientious objector during the Second World War – and it is important to have a knowledge of these influences to fully appreciate the text. In this guide, the **Context** chapter will provide you with information about Jenkins' life and ideas; the historical, social and cultural influences prevalent at the time of the Second World War; and how this background may have shaped the novel. This section can be read before you begin reading the novel and will also be helpful during your revision.

Study and revision

As your reading of the novel progresses, you can refer to this guide's notes on several literary features. The **Study and revision** chapter is divided into four sections: 3.1 Plot and structure, 3.2 Characterisation,

3.3 Themes and 3.4 Language features and analysis. Each section can be read in tandem with the novel or when revising, allowing you to enhance your understanding of these aspects of the text. For example, the section on characterisation contains detailed notes on the main characters; in the plot and structure section, you will find useful synopses of each chapter as well as commentary on key events.

When you have finished reading the novel, Chapter 4: Approaching the Critical Reading paper will provide you with lots of guidance on how to apply your knowledge of the novel in an examination context. This section of the guide will help you with all aspects of revision: it contains everything you need to know about the tasks you will face in the Critical Reading examination paper.

For Scottish text questions, there is specific guidance on successfully decoding and answering the different types of questions you will encounter in the examination. Sample answers to questions are provided and these will give you a clear idea of the level of response needed for success. There are also examination-style questions that give you an opportunity to practise your skills and show off your knowledge of the text.

For critical essay revision, there is detailed guidance on how to 'read' and choose suitable questions, as well as advice on planning and writing effective essays on the novel. Again, there are practice essay questions and samples that will help you to produce your best work.

Some final advice

As you can see, there is a great deal of useful guidance in this book. However, the most important thing to remember is that it is *your* knowledge and understanding of the novel that are being tested. It is therefore important to think carefully about the novel and come up with your own ideas, rather than memorising and rewriting details from this guide. You need to demonstrate that *you* have engaged with the text and that *you* can appreciate Jenkins' craftsmanship. This means that it is always useful to ask yourself questions about the novel as you are reading: you might ask why a character acts in a certain way or how the setting influences a particular event. If you do this, there is no doubt that you will enjoy the novel much more and will be able to answer examination questions much more effectively.

Target your thinking

- What does 'context' mean?
- How did Jenkins' life influence his writing?
- How did political, cultural and historical influences shape Jenkins' creation of the novel?
- Does the novel conform to a particular literary genre?

Glossary

literary context: where the text sits in relation to literary genres or literary traditions and how the writer might have been influenced by other writers and works of literature.

What does 'context' mean?

If you look up the word 'context' in a dictionary, you will probably find a variety of definitions, all of which encapsulate the general idea of 'being related to or connected to something greater'. However, 'context' can also be used in the study of literature – **'literary context'** has a fairly specific definition.

It is often very helpful – and interesting – to think about how the text might have been influenced by events in the writer's life and by the social, cultural and historical background of the text's setting or of the time period during which it was written. You will not have to answer directly on context in the examination but having a knowledge of the novel's context will ensure that you have a greater appreciation of features such as characterisation and theme. You will then be able to respond to Scottish text questions and critical essay questions in far greater depth.

Robin Jenkins's life

▲ Robin Jenkins at his writing desk

Robin Jenkins was born on 11 September 1912 in Cambuslang, on the outskirts of Glasgow. His given name was actually John Jenkins, but he used the name Robin for the publication of his first novel (in 1951) and it became his writing name from that point onwards. His early life was a difficult one. One of four siblings, the premature death of his father when Jenkins was only seven years old meant that the family were no strangers to poverty: perhaps this is one reason why his writing is often concerned with characters who have to endure hardship and poor social conditions.

Fortunately, Jenkins found an escape route by winning a bursary to Hamilton Academy. He was a bright child who did well at school and, with the help of another scholarship, went on to study literature and history at Glasgow University. He graduated in 1936 and married a year later. His political views were left-wing and the onset of the Second World War in 1939 reinforced these views. He registered as a **conscientious objector** as soon as war began.

At that time, conscientious objectors were often ostracised and many were given difficult and dangerous jobs to do. Jenkins was sent to work in forestry operations in Argyll. This was an experience that influenced his writing of *The Cone-Gatherers* – just as the poverty of his childhood influenced many of his other novels. However, he was careful to explain to his readers that although he 'did once gather cones…there was no sinister Duror skulking among the trees', the characters and events of the novel were all a product of his imagination.

After the war, he taught English and history in several Scottish secondary schools, spending time in the East End of Glasgow and at Dunoon Grammar School. His teaching spells in Scotland were interrupted by time spent teaching abroad. He had previously taught in Afghanistan and Spain, and in the 1960s he spent four years teaching in Borneo (accompanied by his wife and children). All of these experiences were a fertile source of inspiration for his writing. On his return to Scotland, he once again taught in Dunoon until his retirement.

Jenkins continued to write throughout his teaching career, producing 30 novels and two collections of short stories. His most famous novel is *The Cone-Gatherers*, which has been praised in Giamatti's introduction as 'a profound exploration of the loneliness, fear and heroism hidden in the ancient heart of Man' (page vii). Many of his other novels have won critical acclaim: *The Changeling*, *Fergus Lamont* and *The Thistle and the Grail* in particular have consolidated his position as a writer of great power and imagination. In 1999, he was awarded the OBE. He was further honoured in 2002 when his contribution to literature and Scottish culture was recognised by the Saltire Society, which awarded him the Andrew Fletcher of Saltoun Award.

On his death in February 2005, he was aged 92. Many people lamented the passing of a writer who was described as 'the greatest Scottish novelist of the modern age'. His novels explore universal concerns such as morality, the conflict of good and evil and the human condition. The literary craftsmanship and great imaginative scope of his writing continue to captivate readers in Scotland and far beyond.

Setting in time and place

The Cone-Gatherers was first published in 1955, some ten years after the Second World War. However, the novel is set during the time of the Second World War (1939–45) and, as previously mentioned, Jenkins had direct experience of forestry work as a conscientious objector during

conscientious objector: a person who refuses to serve in the armed forces or complete military service during wartime because of moral or religious reasons.

the war. The war is the reason for the cone-gatherers' presence on the estate: they have been sent there to gather seed cones from the trees to ultimately replace the forest which is shortly to be cut down for the war effort. The war is a constantly threatening presence in the novel and Jenkins frequently reminds us of the conflict outside the immediate setting of the Runcie-Campbell estate.

▲ Woodland where cones were gathered in Argyll during the Second World War

The geographical setting is the estate of Sir Colin Runcie-Campbell and his wife, Lady Runcie-Campbell. Most of the novel's action takes place in the estate's forest. Occasionally, the setting switches to other parts of the estate: the dismal forest hut where Neil and Calum live; the stately home and gardens of the Runcie-Campbell family; the beach hut belonging to Lady Runcie-Campbell; gamekeeper Duror's house; and the nearby village of Lendrick. The estate lies beside a sea-loch on Scotland's west coast, near to the forest of Ardmore where the cone-gatherers have been working for almost five years.

The setting in time: the Second World War

The Second World War was a time of great hardship across the world and although there is no actual combat in the Argyll setting of the novel, all of the characters are affected by the war. Throughout the novel, there are references to wartime events that are happening in the outside world: Duror's obsessive hatred of deformity leads him to secretly approve of the genocide being perpetrated by the Nazi regime; Tulloch mourns his brother, who has been killed at Dunkirk; Lady Runcie-Campbell wonders whether her husband and brother will survive the war in the North African desert.

One of the major **themes** of the novel is the conflict between good and evil, and this is reflected not only in Duror's obsessive hatred of Calum but also in the far greater conflict that rages in the world outside the estate. On the first page of the novel, Jenkins contrasts the 'homely' beauty of the tree in which Calum and Neil are gathering cones with the nearby and menacing presence of a naval 'destroyer' and 'gunshots' in the woods. We quickly learn that there is no hiding from the conflict: it is a presence that affects the lives of everyone in the novel. By describing the hardships of rationing, the constant fear for family members in the midst of the fighting or the hostility shown to the conscientious objectors working in Ardmore, Jenkins reminds us that the conflict between good and evil is all around us, and that even the most peaceful places are in danger.

Glossary

theme: a central idea or key concern that a writer explores in a text. A theme is a key idea that the writer wants us to think about when reading, or after reading, the text. Themes can be explored through the writer's use of features such as characterisation, plot, structure, language, etc.

The Second World War was also a time when the established hierarchy of social class in Britain underwent a dramatic change. The strict class structures that had existed for centuries were gradually eroding. The war brought great upheavals in Britain's political and economic systems. Like almost all Scottish landowners at that time, Sir Colin Runcie-Campbell is a member of the upper-class aristocracy; he believes that the class structure should be preserved and that his superiority and rights should not be challenged by those of a lower class. Sir Colin's absence because of war service leaves Lady Runcie-Campbell in charge of the estate and she is far less confident in her role as aristocratic land owner. She faces an internal conflict between her desire to uphold her social position and the Christian ideals of looking after the less fortunate in society.

At the other end of the social spectrum are the cone-gatherers. At this period in time, the lowest classes still had very little power. This is made clear when Duror describes the brothers as 'sub-human'. In fact, the brothers' low social position is a cause of a great deal of their suffering and they are often treated with less respect than animals. Neil resents the idea of the restrictive social class structure and represents the views held by many social reformers at that time. Jenkins was a firm believer in social equality and his beliefs are echoed in Neil's desire for a fairer world in which even the poorest members of society have a chance to live comfortably.

Build critical skills

When you have read the novel, think about how the characters are used by Jenkins to show the views of different social classes. Do all of the characters fit neatly into a social class or are some characters more difficult to define socially?

The setting in place: the Runcie-Campbell estate and its surroundings

When Jenkins registered as a conscientious objector, he had to appear before two military tribunals to explain that his objection to military service was on moral rather than religious grounds. At that time, conscientious objectors were employed in various roles: some became army medics; others worked in heavy industry or agriculture. Jenkins was sent to work in forestry in Argyll and his experience during that time contributed to his imaginative creation of the Runcie-Campbell estate and the work of the cone-gatherers.

The novel opens with a description of the forest, which suggests it is a very beautiful place – almost like **Eden**. However, in the same way that Eden was dangerous for the innocent Adam and Eve, the forest is also not as beautiful as it appears. Throughout the novel, Jenkins uses religious **symbolism** to explore the key themes of good and evil, and many of the descriptions of the forest are symbolic in this way. Calum is an innocent character who is associated with the goodness and beauty of nature in the forest, whereas Duror is often associated with the dark and sinister aspects of the forest.

The grand mansion inhabited by the Runcie-Campbell family is another setting that is used effectively by Jenkins to show the power and privilege of the upper classes. The mansion is in direct contrast to the squalor of the cone-gatherers' hut in the forest. Neil is acutely aware of this unfair divide. His bitter comment that the mansion is 'a house with fifty rooms, every one of them three times the size of our hut, and nearly all of them empty' reveals his frustration at the social inequality and humiliation he has to endure. Although the cone-gatherers' hut is shoddy, Calum's simpleminded nature allows him to feel at home there. The hut is often associated with light and warmth from the fire. It becomes a symbol for goodness and innocence in contrast to the darkness of the forest and Duror's dark obsessions.

There are other settings on the estate that are used effectively: Duror's house is used to show his isolation from other characters; the silver fir trees surrounding the mansion and the garden are symbolic of the social barriers that separate upper and lower classes; the beach hut offers only a fleeting chance of comfort to the brothers, thus revealing the hopelessness of their situation. The village of Lendrick is self-contained, yet it also helps to emphasise the fact that war reaches everywhere. When Neil and Calum visit the hotel's pub, they are shamed by the thoughtless joking of a group of soldiers and the hostility shown to the conscientious objectors suggests that conflict and evil exist all around us.

Eden: a paradise. In the biblical account of creation, Eden was the beautiful garden that God created for Adam and Eve to inhabit.

Glossary

symbolism: the use of symbols to represent an idea or a meaning that is not literal. For example, in this novel, Duror's growing insanity is symbolised by 'a tree…tossed by a gale'.

Literary context

The Cone-Gatherers is often described as an **allegory** and sometimes described as a **fable**. Both of these descriptions could be applied to the novel as it deals with moral themes such as the conflict of good and evil, fairness, justice and redemption. Read as an allegory, the conflict between Duror and the brothers could be representative of the struggle between good and evil in the world; Lady Runcie-Campbell's feelings of 'purified hope, and joy' after Calum's death could represent the ideas of sacrifice and redemption. There are certainly layers of meanings within the characters and plot. The novel also contains many elements of the fable **genre**. It has a fairly simple plot that takes place over a short timescale of a few days. It also has an ending which could be read as a moral lesson: that goodness will eventually overcome evil and will provide us with hope.

Glossary

allegory: a text, usually a story, in which the characters and events take on a much deeper moral or political or religious meaning

fable: a short story which provides a moral lesson

genre: in literature, genre means the type, style or category of a text. Plays, novels and poems all belong to separate genres. Texts can also be classified by genres that relate to the style of writing – for example, thrillers or romances

---

REVIEW YOUR LEARNING

(Answers are given on p. 108.)

1 What is meant by the term 'context'?
2 Why did Robin Jenkins work in forestry for some time?
3 When did the Second World War take place?
4 How might smaller communities have been affected by the war?
5 How would people have been affected by social class structure during the Second World War?
6 What does 'symbolism' mean?
7 Name two characters who could be viewed as symbolic and explain what these characters symbolise.
8 What does the term 'allegory' mean?

3.1 Plot and structure

Target your thinking

- What are the main events of the novel?
- How are the main characters affected by key incidents?
- How do these key incidents lead to the climax of the novel?

Plot

The following chapter summaries explore the main events of the novel in more depth.

Chapter 1

The novel begins with the brothers, Neil and Calum, high up in a larch tree in the woods of the Runcie-Campbells' Lendrickmore estate. They have been gathering the cones that will provide seed to replace trees being cut down for the war effort. The younger brother, Calum, is physically disabled – he is described as 'a hunchback' – but is completely at home in the trees and loves nature. Neil, the elder brother, is far less comfortable in the trees than Calum and is deeply dissatisfied with the social divisions and inequality brought on by the class system at that time.

When returning to their impoverished hut that evening, the brothers come across an injured rabbit caught in a snare placed by Duror, the estate's gamekeeper. Calum is deeply distressed at the rabbit's injuries, but his deep compassion will not allow him to end its suffering. Neil insists that they leave the rabbit for Duror, as they have already provoked the gamekeeper's anger by interfering with other snares. Neil also makes it clear that he is not happy with the brothers' short-term removal to the Runcie-Campbell estate, saying that he would far rather be back at Ardmore forest where they normally work.

Unseen by the brothers, Duror watches them with hatred, his gun aimed at Calum. Duror harbours a particular hatred for Calum: he is repelled by Calum's physical deformity and regards the brothers' presence in the woods as a pollution and defilement of a space that had been a refuge for him. Duror follows the brothers as they return to the hut and obsessively watches them for some time. His mental deterioration and inability to accept Calum's physical imperfections are revealed through his secret approval of the Nazis' use of concentration camps. Duror finally leaves, thinking bitterly of the brothers' peaceful lives set against the carnage of the war.

This chapter is important in setting the context of the novel. Immediately, we know that the events are set in a time of war and Neil's complaints also introduce the themes of social inequality and class. The opening chapter also introduces us to the conflicting characters of Calum and Duror, providing a glimpse of Calum's innocence set against Duror's obsession.

Build critical skills

Calum's goodness is established early in this chapter. Write down a list of quotations or actions that show this aspect of Calum's character.

Chapter 2

After leaving his vigil outside the hut, Duror is stopped by Dr Matheson. The doctor drives Duror to the estate gates. The conversation in the car is mostly one-sided, with the doctor hopeful of supplementing his wartime rations with some venison from Duror. Duror is distant throughout the conversation and when the doctor asks about Duror's wife, Peggy, Duror says little. Peggy has been bedridden for 20 years, having been paralysed not long after marrying Duror. In that time, she has 'grown monstrously obese'.

When the doctor drops him off, Duror is reluctant to return to his house. He realises that he is losing control of his mind: Peggy's disability, the frustrations of the past 20 years and his obsessive hatred of deformity have been exacerbated by the arrival of the cone-gatherers in his sole place of refuge. When he reaches the house, he upsets Peggy and her mother, Mrs Lochie, by remaining distant. Peggy loves him and wants him to spend time with her, but he finds it impossible to get over his physical revulsion for her. Her mother keeps house for the couple, but is finding it increasingly difficult to meet the demands of looking after someone with a disability. Duror avoids conflict with both women by going outside to attend to his dogs.

When he learns that Lady Runcie-Campbell wishes to organise a deer hunt for her visiting brother, Duror realises that forcing the cone-gatherers to participate in the hunt could be a means of removing them from the estate. He believes that Calum will become a 'drivelling obscenity' when confronted with a butchered deer and that Lady Runcie-Campbell's disgust will result in the brothers' dismissal.

Key quotation

Duror: 'Hidden among the spruces at the edge of the ride...stood Duror the gamekeeper, in an icy sweat of hatred, with his gun aimed all the time at the feebleminded hunchback grovelling over the rabbit.'

Build critical skills

In Chapter 2, we are given some important details about Duror's life and character. Write down all of the things we learn about Duror.

Chapter 3

Duror's mood is slightly better the next day – perhaps because his plans for the deer hunt offer some hope for his sanity. He sets out early to see Lady Runcie-Campbell, but his unshaven state hints at his gradual deterioration. On reaching the house, he silently watches the Runcie-Campbell family, who are playing cricket on the lawn. Lord Runcie-Campbell is on active service, so the estate is being run by Lady Runcie-Campbell in his absence. The children, Sheila and Roderick, are opposites in nature. Sheila accepts her superior position as a member of the aristocracy, but Roderick is a far more sensitive and imaginative boy who is less comfortable with social inequalities.

Captain Forgan, Lady Runcie-Campbell's brother, is visiting before going to North Africa on wartime service. Duror speaks briefly with him about the deer drive. Captain Forgan becomes aware of Duror's unhappiness and is slightly disturbed by this, although he also feels sorry for him.

Duror continues to the house and has a brief conversation with Mrs Morton, the cook and housekeeper on the estate. Mrs Morton is a widow who admires Duror and has hopes of a future relationship with him in the event of Peggy's death. However, Duror's sexual repression is seen in the disturbing way in which he manipulates their conversation – falsely portraying the innocent Calum as a sexual deviant. He realises that an affair with Effie Morton could offer salvation but rejects this in favour of his plans to ruin the cone-gatherers.

Chapter 4

Duror proceeds to Lady Runcie-Campbell's office to make arrangements for the deer drive. He recognises her goodness and faith in Christian values and he feels some guilt about involving her in his plans to bring about the cone-gatherers' downfall. However, he also plays upon her aristocratic values, encouraging her to coerce Neil and Calum to take part.

Before arranging the beaters for the hunt, Lady Runcie-Campbell tells Duror that the hunting party will consist of her brother, Captain Forgan; the estate's factor, Mr Baird; Mr Adamson; and herself. She then asks Duror for his advice on whether her son, Roderick, should be allowed to take part. Duror is aware that Roderick does not like him and, for a very brief moment, thinks that allowing Roderick to take part offers an 'opportunity' for the boy to have an accident. He decides against this, thinking briefly of the tragedy of his own dead son.

After discussing the hunting party, Duror mentions the 'trouble' with finding enough beaters for the drive. He then puts his scheme into place by suggesting that the cone-gatherers could be used as beaters. Delighted with this suggestion, Lady Runcie-Campbell contacts Tulloch, the Ardmore forester who supervises the cone-gatherers, to formally request Neil and Calum's assistance. She suddenly remembers Calum's disability, but Duror assures her that this will not be an issue. After a short telephone conversation, she secures Tulloch's permission.

The time and place for the deer drive are arranged but just as Duror is about to leave, Tulloch telephones to warn Lady Runcie-Campbell about Calum's love of animals and his aversion to hunting. During the conversation, it is clear that she is torn between her Christian compassion for Calum and her social position as a member of the aristocracy. Duror subtly manipulates the conversation, suggesting that the brothers are fit enough for the drive and have a duty to obey her. She finally decides that Neil and Calum should participate and Duror sets off to tell the brothers of her decision. As he is leaving, she reminds Duror that she will visit Peggy soon.

Chapter 5

That same morning, as Duror is on his way to tell Neil and Calum that they are to serve as beaters for the deer drive, the brothers are happily gathering cones in a tall larch. The sun is shining and both men enjoy the warmth and beauty which surround them. Calum is totally at home in this natural setting, while Neil looks forward to their Saturday visit to the nearby village of Lendrick. The idyllic mood is shattered when Calum notices Duror's approach: his agitation affects Neil, who tries to assure him that there is nothing to fear. Nevertheless, it is clear that Neil also fears Duror's presence.

Duror arrives at the tree and begins to climb the ladder. Neil initially wonders if this is a friendly visit but is alarmed when his attempts to engage Duror in conversation are met with silence. The brothers are in the topmost branches of the tree and cannot see that Duror is overcome by a fear of heights and is temporarily unable to speak.

Neil is shocked when Duror tells him of the deer drive. At first, he argues that Lady Runcie-Campbell is not their employer and has no authority over them, but Duror informs them that Tulloch at Ardmore has agreed to their participation. When Neil then argues that Calum has never had to take part in hunts and that this has to be a 'trick', Duror simply ignores his objections – not mentioning that Tulloch has already expressed his concerns about Calum.

Duror manages to climb down the ladder but is overcome by misery and temporarily loses his grip on reality when he reaches the ground. The touch of his dogs rescues him from thoughts of suicide.

In the tree, Neil is at a loss about what to do. He is acutely worried about the danger the deer drive poses to Calum's physical and mental health. Calum tells Neil that he will take part in the hunt and will do his best to avoid injury or distress.

Build critical skills

Build critical skills

Jenkins presents Lady Runcie-Campbell as a character with a strong internal conflict. What are the elements of this conflict? Write down several examples of where this conflict is made clear.

Build critical skills

We see key differences between Calum's and Neil's characters in this chapter. In what ways do the brothers' views on their lives differ?

Key quotations

Neil: 'Another hindrance had been the constant sight of the mansion house chimneys, reminding him of their hut, which to him remained a symbol of humiliation.'

Duror: 'He was like a tree still straight, still showing green leaves; but underground death was creeping along the roots.'

Chapter 6

At two o'clock that afternoon, the estate workers who are to act as beaters wait by the lily pond for Duror's arrival. The small party consists of Harry, the gardener's apprentice; Betty, a land girl; Erchie Graham, an elderly handyman; and Charlie, one of Mr Adamson's labourers. While waiting for the arrival of the cone-gatherers and Duror, they are shaken by Duror stumbling out of the shrubbery and calling out his wife's name.

Duror seems incoherent and unable to focus clearly on his surroundings or the task at hand. The beaters are puzzled by this transformation: Duror is usually completely in control, but his unkempt appearance and mumbled commands are suggestive of an illness. The truth is that Duror has just awakened from a terrible dream in which he watches as Peggy is pecked to death by hundreds of thrushes.

The arrival of the cone-gatherers draws attention away from Duror's unusual behaviour. Neil instantly states that he and Calum will participate only if Calum is given a clear stretch of the woods. Duror remains remote from this discussion, but the other beaters readily agree. At the end of this conversation, Duror unexpectedly laughs and sets off at a fast pace. Graham warns Neil and Calum to keep out of sight of the guns.

The deer drive begins in earnest, with the beaters giving different cries as they work their way through the woods. The innocent Calum is entranced by the beauty of the woods, while Neil endures the difficult terrain. Near the end, Calum spots some deer and realises that the guns and dogs are nearby. In a blind panic, he sets out after the deer in a futile bid to protect them. One of the animals is wounded and Calum desperately tries to comfort and protect it, completely unaware of the danger he faces.

The rest of the shooting party look on in horror and are then shocked by the sight of Duror, who gleefully throws Calum from the deer and cuts the animal's throat. Duror's frenzied behaviour ceases as soon as the deer dies. When Tulloch goes to check if Duror has been injured, the gamekeeper asks for his wife. Lady Runcie-Campbell, aware that Duror is ill in some way, tells him that he should see a doctor.

Meanwhile, Tulloch has spoken to the brothers and has learned that they have been forced into the deer hunt by Duror. He agrees to speak up for them with Lady Runcie-Campbell and tells them that she is fair-minded. Tulloch feels great sympathy for Neil and Calum, and he attempts to prevent the furious Lady Runcie-Campbell from ejecting them from the woods. Roderick also stands up for the brothers. Lady Runcie-Campbell asks for Duror's opinion, but the gamekeeper is unable to speak. Her brother's statement that Calum's behaviour has not upset his memories of that day finally convinces her that Calum and Neil should be allowed to continue working in the woods.

Key quotations

Calum: 'Calum was no longer one of the beaters; he too was a deer hunted by remorseless men.'
Duror: 'For many years his life had been stunted, misshapen, obscene, and hideous; and this misbegotten creature was its personification.'

Build critical skills

Think about Lady Runcie-Campbell's different emotions at the end of the deer drive. Write down an explanation for each emotion she experiences.

Chapter 7

On the Saturday of that week, the brothers spend the morning gathering cones. Neil is bitter and resentful at their situation and is unwilling to feel thankful that Lady Runcie-Campbell has allowed the brothers to remain in the woods. On the walk back to their hut at lunchtime, he takes his anger out on Calum, chastising him for his innocent acceptance of their lowly status. Calum cannot understand Neil's resentment of the class system or the responsibilities Neil has to shoulder.

At lunchtime, the brothers eat the meagre remains of their weekly provisions and prepare to visit the village of Lendrick. Neil's mood improves at the thought of the visit. The brothers catch the bus with high hopes for a good day.

In Lendrick, everyone greets them with kindness and courtesy. The local policeman, draper and grocer chat affably with Neil and Calum, the grocer generously providing some extra provisions. They admire a small steamer in the harbour and Neil daydreams of his wish to go to sea. While Neil is watching the comings and goings in the harbour, Calum slips off to buy him a gift of a new pipe.

In the café, they are given large portions and treated kindly by the staff who know them well and treat them differently to the Ardmore men who are conscientious objectors. Neil and Calum feel slightly awkward at the differing ways in which the conscientious objectors are treated; at Ardmore, they have worked with these men and have come to like them. Neil feels guilty as he conforms to the Lendrick folk's offhand treatment of these workers. Nevertheless, his desire to feel accepted in the community overcomes his unease at being less tolerant than he usually would be at Ardmore.

On leaving the café, the brothers' good mood is spoiled by the sight of the Runcie-Campbells' car. An agitated Calum wishes to avoid walking past the car, but Neil insists that there is nothing to be afraid of. When Roderick greets the brothers, Neil feels awkward and socially inferior.

> **Build critical skills**
>
> The wartime setting is made clear in Chapter 7. Make a note of all the references to this time period and note the way in which the conscientious objectors are treated.

Chapter 8

Lady Runcie-Campbell has come to town with Roderick, Sheila and Duror. She has made an appointment for Duror to see Dr Matheson while she visits the cinema with the children. Her initial surprise at Roderick's greeting to the cone-gatherers is replaced by concern when he explains that he wanted to apologise to them after the events of the deer drive. She is distressed at Roderick's disregard for the social hierarchy but realises that her own Christian values may have led to Roderick's compassion for, and generosity to, others.

When Roderick suggests giving the men a lift home that night, she and her daughter Sheila are outraged and she asks Duror for his opinion. Duror does not hesitate to advise against this and when Roderick protests that his hard-heartedness is out of spite, Duror once again manipulates Lady Runcie-Campbell's view of the cone-gatherers by suggesting he knows something disturbing about Calum. Roderick refuses to believe that Calum is evil, but Lady Runcie-Campbell tells Duror that they will discuss this accusation later.

Duror, aware that he is physically fit but that his mind is deteriorating, visits Dr Matheson. He takes with him a gift of venison from Lady Runcie-Campbell: watching the doctor's greedy delight, he realises that he is unlikely to receive any help from him. The doctor subjects Duror to a thorough physical examination but also asks questions about his faith, his marriage and his mental endurance. During this conversation, Duror again lies about Calum and implies that the disabled cone-gatherer is a sexual pervert. Dr Matheson ignores these accusations and defends Calum, and it is clear that he is aware of Duror's own repression and mental instability. The doctor's final advice to Duror is to remain patient and endure.

Chapter 9

Duror finally manages to leave the doctor's surgery after patiently listening to the doctor's complaints and drinking too much whisky. He is in a black and violent frame of mind, and once again contemplates suicide as he stands at the harbour's edge. On entering the hotel bar, he reflects on the bleakness of his marriage and realises that there is no hope in his life.

He catches sight of the cone-gatherers and, although assuming an air of involvement in the conversation around him, is unable to draw his thoughts away from Calum. In Duror's mind, Calum has become the personification of everything that has gone wrong in his life, and all of his frustration and hatred is concentrated on the younger brother.

Duror's obsessive regard of Calum and Neil is interrupted by the arrival of a party of soldiers, one of whom is in particularly high spirits and begins to tell jokes. Unfortunately, he begins to tell a joke about a pilot with a pet ape, before spotting Calum's disability as the brothers try to leave discreetly. Stricken with remorse over the unintended slight, the soldier apologises to the brothers and soon leaves the bar with his colleagues. The remaining men in the bar share some rumours about Calum and Neil's tragic family circumstances, but the gossip ends with general agreement that the brothers are decent men. In an even bleaker mood, Duror leaves the bar.

Key quotation

Duror: 'The result was a revulsion against the doctor's reiterated philosophy of endurance; indeed... he felt in a mood for murder, rape or suicide.'

Chapter 10

Lady Runcie-Campbell pays a visit to Duror's wife, Peggy. She feels deeply uncomfortable visiting her, but sees the visit as a Christian duty as well as her social duty as a member of the ruling class. On her way to Duror's house, she thinks of her husband's disappointment at Roderick's equal treatment of all social classes, and she realises that Roderick's sense of social justice has come from her father's strong principles and her own Christian values.

The visit to Peggy has a negative effect on Lady Runcie-Campbell's mood and when she returns to the house, she is irritable and finds fault with everything. Roderick plans to visit the cone-gatherers, taking a cake as a peace offering, so he lies to his mother and asks for her permission to go to the beach with Harry. She consents to this and asks to speak privately with Mrs Morton, the housekeeper. As Roderick is leaving the room, Mrs Morton enters and agrees to provide a cake for his trip. Lady Runcie-Campbell asks the housekeeper if she has noticed any change in Duror. The women discuss Duror's allegations about Calum.

Roderick collects the cake and goes to find Harry, but discovers that Harry has gone off to gather hazelnuts. Glad to be unaccompanied, he sets off for the cone-gatherers' hut, imagining himself on a pilgrimage. Like Calum, Roderick is deeply sensitive to the beauty of the natural world and he ignores an opportunity to answer the calls of Harry and Betty, choosing instead to continue his pilgrimage to the hut. He believes that the cake will be a gesture of friendship which offers redemption after the events of the deer hunt.

The forest is a less friendly place, however, and when he nears the hut, he is intimidated and exhausted. Alert to the darkness around him, he spots Duror lurking within the dark cypress tree and intent on watching the hut. Roderick is afraid of Duror and takes refuge in a yew tree. In his confused and miserable state, he recognises that Duror's relationship with the cone-gatherers represents the struggle between good and evil. In his imagination, he sees Duror shooting the brothers. After a considerable time, Duror abandons his vigil, and a stunned and horrified Roderick realises that he has seen true evil. In despair, Roderick returns home, leaving the cake to be eaten by insects.

Build critical skills

In Chapter 10, Jenkins uses Roderick's perceptions of the forest to show contrasting aspects of nature. Make a note of these differing aspects and write down some of the descriptions Jenkins uses to show this contrast.

Chapter 11

Neil and Calum are gathering cones in a tall larch and watching an approaching storm. The brothers are in conflicting moods: Calum is excited by the storm, but Neil is miserable because of his arthritis. The storm breaks and Neil realises that they should have retreated much earlier. Calum associates the lightning with their mother in heaven and Neil, an unbeliever, grows angry with his brother.

The storm is so fierce that Neil believes they will be killed trying to return through the woods to their hut, so he suggests they take refuge in the much nearer beach hut. At first, Calum is reluctant to go there as he fears Lady Runcie-Campbell's anger, but Neil convinces him by telling him that they will leave the hut as they found it.

The brothers gain entry to the hut through an unlocked window and light a fire to warm themselves. Neil observes bitterly that the brothers should have been quartered in the beach hut rather than the hovel in which they have been living. Calum is delighted when he finds children's drawings and toys, and he offers to repair a doll with a missing leg. Neil tells him to leave the doll and the brothers settle to dry their clothes.

However, their relief is short-lived as, after only a few minutes, Lady Runcie-Campbell and the children arrive to shelter from the storm. The family are wet and cold, and Lady Runcie-Campbell is shocked to find the cone-gatherers in the hut. Furious, she asks the brothers to explain their presence. A miserable Neil is so defeated by her class and anger that he cannot answer. It is Calum who speaks up, explaining that Neil was trying to save him. Lady Runcie-Campbell is alarmed by Calum, seeing him as somehow less than human, but Neil still cannot speak up in their defence. The brothers put on their jackets and leave the hut, feeling ashamed, while Lady Runcie-Campbell warns them that there will be consequences.

After the brothers have left, she tells the children that she will speak to Tulloch and the cone-gatherers will be ordered to leave the woods by the end of that week. Roderick is upset at the injustice shown to Neil and Calum. He eventually joins his mother and sister at the fire built by the brothers. His mother decides she will have to speak to Roderick about his scruples.

Build critical skills

Note Lady Runcie-Campbell's treatment of the cone-gatherers and Neil's reaction to her words. Why do you think Neil cannot defend himself?

Chapter 12

On the day following the storm, Tulloch goes to see the cone-gatherers. Neil has telephoned him after the storm, pleading that the brothers be allowed to leave the Lendrickmore woods. Tulloch keeps an open mind on the situation and phones Lady Runcie-Campbell that morning to gain more information. She tells him of the beach hut incident and says she has not yet decided on a course of action. She also agrees to speak with him that afternoon.

On the way to see the cone-gatherers, Tulloch comes across Neil and is shocked by the way in which he has been affected by the dampness and the physical demands of cone-gathering. Distraught, Neil pours out all of his worries and grievances to Tulloch, who agrees to speak to Lady Runcie-Campbell but also reminds Neil that she has to shoulder the responsibilities of her class and conform to a code of behaviour. Tulloch tells him he will ask her to release the cone-gatherers back to Ardmore, replacing them with two of the conscientious objectors. The men take their tea-break together and Tulloch talks about his early life on his family's croft.

Key quotation
Neil: 'Why is it, Mr Tulloch,' he asked, 'that the innocent have always to be sacrificed?'

Chapter 13

Lady Runcie-Campbell is worried about Roderick and struggles with her decision to remove the cone-gatherers from the woods. She cannot understand Roderick's sense of social justice or his attitude to Neil and Calum, and she tells him that people of their class have to conform to the social behaviour expected of them. Roderick, recovered from illness following the storm, seems strangely happy and she wonders why he has changed so suddenly. The doctor confirms that Roderick is perfectly healthy.

At lunch-time, she telephones Duror's house to enlist his aid for the cone-gatherers' departure. Mrs Lochie answers and tells her that Duror's behaviour has been extremely alarming: he has been foul-mouthed and has been carrying an unclothed doll. She attempts to reassure Mrs Lochie, telling her that she will speak to Duror that afternoon. When Lady Runcie-Campbell ends the conversation, she decides not to become involved in Duror's predicament, but she then realises that all human beings are connected and that, as another mortal being, she cannot avoid becoming involved.

Build critical skills

Roderick's views on social class differ dramatically from those of his mother. Make notes on their differing beliefs on class and equality.

Chapter 14

Later that morning, Tulloch helps Neil and Calum for a short while. He has taken them to Scour Point, a sunnier part of the forest beside the loch. He discusses with Neil final arrangements for leaving the forest and sets off for his appointment with Lady Runcie-Campbell. On the way, he meets Roderick who tells him that he would like to speak with the cone-gatherers before they leave. Tulloch tries to discourage him, but eventually relents in the face of Roderick's disappointment. Roderick asks Tulloch about the silver firs beside the house.

Lady Runcie-Campbell is waiting for Tulloch outside the house. They briefly discuss families before she tells him of her decision to dismiss Neil and Calum. She agrees that the brothers can remain until Saturday. Tulloch then asks if she is willing to accept conscientious objectors as replacements for Neil and Calum. While she is thinking about this, Duror arrives. She notices his unkempt appearance and is so disturbed by him that she is secretly relieved at Tulloch's presence.

Duror is holding the doll that Calum found in the beach hut. He speaks incoherently and tells Lady Runcie-Campbell and Tulloch that he found it in Calum's bed, and that Calum has been committing obscene acts with the doll. Shocked, she orders him to be quiet and tells him to go home. He replies that he has work to do and, sensing something evil within him, she insists on his departure. When he has gone, Tulloch tells her that Calum would only have taken the doll to repair it: he warns her that Duror is mentally ill, but he cannot explain why. Lady Runcie-Campbell seems aware that Duror's miserable home life and repression are contributory factors in his mental deterioration, but she cannot speak of this with Tulloch.

Before Tulloch leaves the estate, he wonders whether he should try to take Neil and Calum away before Saturday.

Chapter 15

Lady Runcie-Campbell goes into the house to see Sheila, feeling guilty that she has ordered her daughter indoors after witnessing Duror's disturbed state of mind. She is unwilling to explain Duror's state of mind to Sheila and feels frustrated that her husband's absence forces her to deal with the escalating situation. Mrs Morton interrupts their conversation to inform her of Harry's news that Roderick has climbed one of the very tall silver firs and cannot get down. In disbelief, Lady Runcie-Campbell insists on hearing the story from Harry and then treats him harshly when he hesitantly suggests that Roderick cannot descend because he may have grown afraid at such a great height.

She sends Mrs Morton to fetch Mr Baird and Mr Hendry (the gardener), and races off to the tree with Sheila. They meet the elderly Graham, the handyman, who has only managed to climb 6 metres (20 feet) before having to descend. Roderick is at a height of 27 metres (90 feet), near the top of the tree, and has been gathering cones to take to the cone-gatherers. She suddenly realises that Calum's climbing ability could save Roderick, so sends Graham to fetch the brothers.

Chapter 16

Graham sets off quickly to fetch Calum and Neil. He finds the brothers working at the loch side – Neil on the ground and Calum in a pine tree – and tells them that they are to come and rescue Roderick. Neil, still resentful of the way in which Lady Runcie-Campbell has treated them, refuses to help. He tells Graham that they are not servants, and that she should come and ask for their help herself if she wishes it. Graham tries to reason with Neil, telling him that Roderick is a good boy who is well liked by all, but Neil remains adamant.

Build critical skills

Lady Runcie-Campbell seems to realise that Roderick's predicament is 'the time of crisis', which the events of the past few days have been leading to. What narrative threads have led to this point in the novel?

Returning to tell Lady Runcie-Campbell of Neil's refusal, Graham meets Duror standing alone in the woods. He tells Duror what has happened and is startled by Duror's strange expression. Duror says nothing but stalks off in the direction of the cone-gatherers. Graham warns him that they are free men who cannot be forced into doing something against their will.

To his dismay, Graham finds that Roderick has not yet been rescued and that he will have to pass on the cone-gatherers' message to Lady Runcie-Campbell. Roderick is being comforted by Harry and Manson, a ploughboy, who are taking turns to ascend the lower reaches of the fir. The returning Graham tells Lady Runcie-Campbell that Duror has gone to see the brothers and she reacts with horror, asking if Duror has his gun.

After making sure that Harry and Manson will look after Roderick in the tree, she sets off to ask for the cone-gatherers' help. In her desperate rush for help, she thinks over her treatment of the brothers, her servants and her family – but she is unable to find resolution for the conflict between her class and her religion.

As she gets near to the pine tree where Neil and Calum are working, she hears a gunshot and prays that Duror has not hurt the cone-gatherers. She then sees a devastated Duror walking through the pines. Her gaze shifts to Calum, who is caught in one of the trees by the strap of his cone bag. Shot by Duror, he dangles in the tree: cones tumble from his bag and drops of his blood fall to the forest floor. In desperation, Neil tries to reach his dead brother. In Lady Runcie-Campbell's mind, the scene is reminiscent of the crucifixion.

As she views this horrific scene with Mr Baird, they hear another gunshot and realise that Duror has killed himself. They stand in horrified silence until Sheila's voice reaches them, telling them that Harry has helped Roderick down from the tree. Lady Runcie-Campbell does not immediately react to this, and surprises Mr Baird by falling to her knees beside the cones and Calum's spilt blood. She is unable to pray but instead weeps for Calum's death as a sacrifice that brings new hope.

Key quotations

Duror: 'He was walking away among the pine trees with so infinite a desolation in his every step…'
Lady Runcie-Campbell: 'She could not pray, but she could weep; and as she wept pity, and purified hope, and joy, welled up in her heart.'

REVIEW YOUR LEARNING

(Answers are given on p. 108.)

1   In Chapter 1, what reasons does Neil provide for his belief that he and Calum have been unfairly treated?
2   What factors have contributed to Duror's deterioration?
3   What image is used to describe Duror at various points in the novel?
4   Name the beaters and hunters who take part in the deer drive.
5   What is Calum's hobby?
6   Who eventually rescues Roderick from the silver fir?

Glossary

climax: the point in a narrative when tension or conflict is often at its highest and which comes just before this tension is resolved.

omniscient: all-seeing; having the ability to know everything, including the thoughts of others.

Glossary

denouement: the final section of a story, in which the various threads of a plot are drawn together to a resolution or a final explanation.

Structure

The Cone-Gatherers has a fairly straightforward structure, with the main action taking place over the relatively short time period of several days. The story is divided into 16 chapters, numbered and without titles or headings, which follow the chronological sequence of events leading to the tragic **climax** of the novel. The entire novel is written from the viewpoint of an **omniscient** third person, i.e. a narrator who is 'outside' the events and who can 'see' everything that happens. At times, this narrative style allows us to see the thoughts and the points of view of various characters. This method of narration allows readers to gain a better understanding of characters and their motivations.

The simple chronological structure revolves around three key incidents, with each incident escalating Duror's mental deterioration and deepening his hatred of the cone-gatherers.

THE THREE KEY INCIDENTS

1   The deer drive (Chapter 6).
2   The brothers' retreat to the beach hut during the storm and their subsequent ejection from the hut by Lady Runcie-Campbell (Chapter 11).
3   Roderick's unwise decision to climb a tree from which he cannot climb down (Chapter 15).

These incidents all lead to the **denouement** and climax of the novel (Chapter 16): Duror's murder of Calum, his suicide and the resolution of the conflict within Lady Runcie-Campbell.

Although all of the main characters are involved in the action surrounding these incidents, Duror's madness and hatred of Calum and Neil is the narrative thread that links the events. Duror's irrational need to drive the brothers from the woods – which he views as his 'stronghold and sanctuary' – leads to him forcing them to be beaters in the deer hunt; to his false and disturbing accusations when Calum innocently removes the doll from the beach hut; and to Calum's eventual murder.

There is a cyclical and symbolic nature to the novel's structure: the narrative opens and closes in the woods, with Calum in the trees he loves so much and Duror a constantly menacing presence. The opening and closing chapters both contain reminders of the wartime devastation in the wider world: in the opening chapter we are told of a 'destroyer…steaming seawards', fighter planes which had 'shot down from the sky' and gunshots from nearby military training. The cyclical structure is effectively used by Jenkins to reflect the thematic concerns of regeneration within nature and the endless conflict between good and evil.

The chronological timeline

A timeline for the main events of the novel is outlined in the table below.

Chapter	Timing	What happens
1	A late afternoon and evening, one week after the brothers' arrival in the woods	Neil and Calum complete their day's cone-gathering and return to their hut. They are watched by the menacing Duror. Calum wishes to help a snared rabbit, but Neil will not allow this as Duror could have the brothers dismissed for interfering. Duror seems obsessed with removing the cone-gatherers from the woods.
2	Later the same evening	Duror meets Dr Matheson on the way home. The doctor realises that Duror's life is difficult with a disabled wife and he feels sympathy for him. Duror returns home but spends little time with his wife, Peggy, and her mother. He learns of the planned deer drive and decides to use this against Calum and Neil.
3	The morning of the following day	Duror meets members of the Runcie-Campbell family on his way to see Lady Runcie-Campbell. They are puzzled by his unshaven appearance but are unaware of his increasingly disturbed mental state. He then spreads malignant rumours about Calum.
4	That same morning	Duror visits Lady Runcie-Campbell to make arrangements for the deer hunt. He successfully manipulates the conversation to ensure that the cone-gatherers participate in the deer drive.
5	Later that morning	The cone-gatherers are happily picking cones high up in a larch tree. Duror arrives to tell them they are to take part in the deer drive. Calum is desperately afraid as Duror climbs the ladder on their tree. Unknown to the brothers, Duror is overcome by a fear of heights. However, he delivers the order from Lady Runcie-Campbell. Neil tries to argue but is afraid of the consequences that could come with refusal.
6	The afternoon of the same day – the deer drive **Key incident**	The waiting beaters are startled by Duror, who has awakened from a nightmare in which Peggy is killed. The brothers join the deer drive and Calum tries to help an injured deer. In a frenzy, Duror cuts the deer's throat, seemingly confusing the animal with his wife. Lady Runcie-Campbell decides to remove the brothers from the woods but relents after Tulloch and her son stand up for Neil and Calum.
7	Saturday of the same week	The brothers visit Lendrick village after spending the morning gathering cones. Neil's mood improves as the villagers treat them with courtesy and kindness. However, an encounter with the Runcie-Campbells destroys the brothers' good mood.
8	Later that Saturday afternoon	Lady Runcie-Campbell and the children are in Lendrick to visit the cinema. They bring Duror to see Dr Matheson. The doctor pronounces Duror physically fit but is aware of Duror's mental torment. He can offer no help other than advising Duror to remain patient and put up with life's difficulties.

Chapter	Timing	What happens
9	Saturday evening	Duror leaves the doctor's house and goes to the hotel bar in despair. He sees the cone-gatherers and feels nothing but hatred. His thoughts are interrupted by a party of soldiers, one of whom insensitively tells a joke about an ape but then sees Calum and apologises. The cone-gatherers leave. Duror leaves shortly after them.
10	Sunday morning	Lady Runcie-Campbell goes to visit Duror's wife and finds the visit difficult. Roderick asks his mother if he can go to the beach with Harry, but he really plans to visit the cone-gatherers. He intends to apologise for the deer hunt and takes a cake for them. However, his plans are ruined when he sees Duror obsessively watching the hut. Shocked after hours of observing Duror's malice, Roderick returns home in despair.
11	One day during the following week **Key incident**	The brothers are gathering cones when they are caught in a terrible storm. They flee to the beach hut for safety and warmth but are found there by Lady Runcie-Campbell and her children, who also arrive to take shelter. Furious, she sends them out into the rain. Roderick feels sympathy for the men and is disturbed by his mother's and sister's actions.
12	The day after the storm	Tulloch comes to speak to the cone-gatherers after Neil has telephoned him asking to be taken away from Lendrickmore. He is sympathetic to both Lady Runcie-Campbell and the brothers and says that he will ask her to release the men back to Ardmore.
13	That same morning	Lady Runcie-Campbell speaks to Roderick about his social views, telling him that he should act in a way that befits his higher social class. Roderick avoids direct confrontation and is strangely happy. The doctor visits and confirms Roderick's good health. Lady Runcie-Campbell then telephones to make an appointment with Duror. His mother-in-law answers and tells her that Duror's behaviour is frightening.
14	Early afternoon of the same day	Tulloch helps Neil and Calum to work in a nicer part of the forest before going to see Lady Runcie-Campbell. They agree that the cone-gatherers will leave on Saturday. Duror appears, clutching the doll from the beach hut and accusing Calum of committing obscene acts with it. Lady Runcie-Campbell sends him away. She and Tulloch discuss Duror's increasingly erratic behaviour and his inexplicable hatred of Calum.
15	Later that afternoon **Key incident**	While speaking to Sheila, Lady Runcie-Campbell is interrupted by Mrs Morton who tells her that Roderick is stuck high up in one of the silver fir trees. On arriving at the tree, she sees that Roderick has been collecting cones. She sends Graham to fetch the brothers, thinking that they will be able to rescue Roderick from such a height.

Chapter	Timing	What happens
16	The same afternoon **Climax**	Graham goes to find Calum and Neil. He reaches them and gives them Lady Runcie-Campbell's order. Neil refuses, telling him that they are free men and that she will have to come and ask them herself if she wants help. Graham meets Duror on his return to the silver fir. He tells Duror what has happened and Duror strides off without a word. Graham returns to the silver fir and passes on the brothers' message, mentioning that he has also spoken to Duror. A fearful Lady Runcie-Campbell runs to ask Neil and Calum for help. As she reaches Scour Point, she hears a gunshot and sees Duror walk away. He has shot Calum, whose body is now caught up in the pine tree. Another shot is heard and she realises that Duror has taken his own life. Meanwhile, Roderick has been helped down from the tree by Harry. Lady Runcie-Campbell kneels and begins to weep.

3.2 Characterisation

Target your thinking

- Who are the main characters in *The Cone-Gatherers*?
- How do the characters interact with each other?
- What is the difference between character and characterisation?

Who's who in *The Cone-Gatherers*?

We are introduced to, arguably, the novel's three most important characters in the opening chapter, where Jenkins provides us with a vivid picture of Neil and Calum McPhie's humility set against Duror's malevolence. In that same chapter, we also gain a small amount of information on the Runcie-Campbell family as well as on Tulloch. Almost all of the characters have entered the story by the end of Chapter 6, with only minor characters such as the Lendrick villagers and Manson, the ploughboy, making an appearance later in the novel.

Jenkins uses **characterisation** to bring his characters to life in our imagination and to help us understand why they react to certain situations or settings.

> **Glossary**
>
> **characterisation:** the means by which a writer represents characters in a literary work, i.e. how the writer provides us with information to let us 'see' what a character is like. Characterisation can be direct, where the narrator tells us something about a character, or indirect, where we have to infer something from the character's reactions or actions towards other characters.

Build critical skills

From your reading of the novel, write down the names of any characters who have a symbolic role and state what each character symbolises.

Characters may also have a symbolic role and can be used to convey theme(s). In *The Cone-Gatherers*, Jenkins uses characterisation to present several characters as symbols: for example, Calum's innocent nature symbolises goodness, whereas Duror's unreasoning hatred and malice symbolise evil.

THE CAST OF CHARACTERS (IN ORDER OF APPEARANCE)

- Calum McPhie – a cone-gatherer who is physically deformed but has an angelic face and an innocent nature.
- Neil McPhie – Calum's elder brother. He has looked after Calum since the death of their mother.
- John Duror – the gamekeeper on the Lendrickmore estate. He is employed by the aristocratic Runcie-Campbell family.
- Dr Matheson – the local doctor.
- Mrs Lochie – Duror's mother-in-law. She looks after Duror's disabled wife, Peggy, and is housekeeper to the couple.
- Captain Forgan – Lady Runcie-Campbells' brother. He is upper-class and is visiting his sister before he begins wartime service in North Africa.
- Roderick Runcie-Campbell – Sir Colin and Lady Runcie-Campbell's only son, and the heir to the title and Lendrickmore estate.
- Sheila Runcie-Campbell – Sir Colin and Lady Runcie-Campbell's only daughter.
- Mrs Morton – the Runcie-Campbells' housekeeper and cook.
- Lady Runcie-Campbell – the wife of Sir Colin Runcie-Campbell. She is custodian of the estate while her husband is on active service in North Africa.
- Tulloch – the head forester at the nearby Ardmore estate. He has arranged for Neil and Calum to gather cones at Lendrickmore and is sympathetic to the brothers' situation.
- Erchie Graham – an elderly handyman on the Lendrickmore estate.
- Mr Baird – the farm manager for the Runcie-Campbells.
- Harry – the gardener's apprentice.
- Betty – a land girl.
- Mr Adamson of Ledaig – Lady Runcie-Campbell's friend and neighbour.
- Various villagers in Lendrick.

Main characters

Duror

▲ A gamekeeper making his way home – a lonely job at times

Initial view

Duror is perhaps the most complex character in the novel, and his mental deterioration is the narrative 'thread' that links the other characters and events. For this reason, all of Duror's actions could be considered as significant to the novel's plot.

Duror is a gamekeeper, employed by the titled and land-owning Runcie-Campbell family. As a gamekeeper, his role is to manage the wildlife on the estate as well as overseeing hunting, shooting and fishing activities. Gamekeepers at that time would have been well respected by other servants on the estate and Duror certainly seems to command respect from various characters. However, despite his initial appearance of control, it is clear that he is struggling to hold back the frustrations that have plagued him for so long. We quickly realise that his obsession with the cone-gatherers is an indication of the mental instability overtaking him.

His thoughts and deterioration

We first see Duror when he is watching the two cone-gatherers 'in an icy sweat of hatred' and it is clear that there is something deeply wrong with him. Throughout the novel, he is a malignant presence filled with an inexplicable hatred. This hatred is concentrated on Calum, but it also encompasses other characters. In the opening chapter, we see Duror lost in a fantasy of the cone-gatherers' deaths as he imagines them falling from the tree. He keeps his gun aimed at them as he silently watches Calum's concern for the trapped rabbit, but it quickly becomes apparent that his hatred is not simply caused by Calum's previous release of rabbits from snares.

To the reader, Duror's extreme reaction to the kind and simple Calum's distress is shocking and puzzling. It is even more confusing when we learn that Duror is aware of the despair and dark thoughts that threaten him: Jenkins uses direct characterisation in showing these thoughts: '...the last obscene squeal of the killed dwarf would have been for him, he thought, release too, from the noose of disgust and despair drawn, these past few days, so much tighter.' For Duror, Calum personifies everything that is wrong with his life and this is one of the reasons why he has such spite against the innocent little cone-gatherer.

There are several other reasons for Duror's final deterioration. The first of these is 'the silent tribulation of the past twenty years', which is how Duror thinks of his marriage to Peggy, who was paralysed soon after they wed. Duror is also repelled by any kind of physical deformity, so has a pathological hatred of both Peggy, who we are told is 'monstrously obese', and the 'hunchback'. The arrival of the cone-gatherers, who now live in the woods that were Duror's only place of refuge, sparks his determination to have them removed. Neil and Calum's presence is the final circumstance in a chain of events which unleashes Duror's pent-up frustrations and rage.

Other characters' views

Jenkins allows us to gain insight into different aspects of Duror's character and motivations by letting us see not only Duror's thoughts but also the other characters' view of Duror. It is clear that Duror has been well regarded on the estate and in the local community. In fact, the only character who seems initially critical of Duror is his mother-in-law, Mrs Lochie: her early recognition of Duror's flaws is likely a result of witnessing his revulsion for Peggy and the repression that accompanies this. The other characters seem to admire Duror's endurance in coping with the misfortunes of his domestic life and there is no indication that they see him as a monster in the making.

Although aware of Duror's social inferiority, Lady Runcie-Campbell asks Duror for advice at several points in the novel. It is clear that she trusts his judgement and takes his experience into account in the absence of Sir Colin. Yet Duror takes advantage of this trust when making plans for the cone-gatherers' destruction. It is only when an almost incoherent Duror appears with the naked doll that Lady Runcie-Campbell, although still 'feeling a strange, remote, sterile pity' for the gamekeeper, begins to doubt Duror's sanity. Her decision not to involve herself is a contributory factor in Duror's downfall.

Key quotation

Duror: 'He had read that the Germans were putting idiots and cripples to death in gas chambers. Outwardly, as everybody expected, he condemned such barbarity; inwardly... he had profoundly approved.'

Build critical skills

Make a note of the sections of the novel where Lady Runcie-Campbell asks for Duror's advice.

The final tragedy

By the end of the novel, the scene is set for the final tragedy. Duror's fate is unavoidable. He can find no comfort in the woods or at the elm tree which has for so long offered reassurance – even his loyal dogs are uneasy, sensing the rage and frustration within him. Indeed, when Duror interrupts a conversation between his mistress and Tulloch, Lady Runcie-Campbell is startled to see Duror without his dogs. Although she does not fear him, she recognises his potential for evil and sends him from her presence, afraid that she might be caught up in the 'gruesome other world' where he now exists.

It seems inevitable that Duror will take out his rage and madness on Calum, but even after his murder, it is possible to feel some sympathy for Duror. The destruction of Calum brings no relief to Duror, only further 'desolation' and no hope for himself. Although Jenkins portrays Duror as the symbol of evil, contrasting with Calum's goodness, we see that evil cannot win in this battle. Jenkins uses the imagery of Christ's crucifixion to suggest regeneration and rebirth will arise from Duror's actions. For Duror, however, there is no hope – only his own death can remove the evil that has become a part of him. When he kills himself and Calum, Lady Runcie-Campbell weeps because she understands that evil has been vanquished and hope can return to Lendrickmore.

Calum

His goodness

Both as a character and a symbol, Calum is the **antithesis** of Duror. He is a totally innocent character whose goodness is apparent throughout the novel. We first meet Calum in the treetops where he is most at home and his connection to nature is clear. His goodness is established in the description of the chaffinches that flutter around him yet ignore his brother. The comparison with St Francis of Assisi, a good and humble man who was said to converse with the birds, suggests that Calum is wholly good. Although working on gathering cones, he is entranced by the natural world around him and his 'beautiful' face adds to the impression of an angelic persona. It is interesting to note that, unlike his brother Neil, Calum has no thoughts of the war, class system or everyday burdens: this adds to our impression of an almost mystical character who is removed from the ordinary world.

In the trees, Calum is at home, but he is far less so when he has to return to earth; this is also suggestive of his angelic qualities. His physical appearance is certainly not that of an angel – we are told of the curvature of his spine and stumbling gait – and he is compared to an ape at several points. However, Calum's physical deformities are not

antithesis: the direct opposite or contrast of an idea, person or object.

33

reflected in his nature: although Neil describes him as 'simple' and he is unable to comprehend the issues that vex Neil, Calum has no bitterness of the soul. He delights in being kind to others: buying Neil a pipe; making friends with the shunned conscientious objectors at Ardmore; making a carved squirrel for Tulloch's baby daughter. He even manages to speak up in Neil's defence when Lady Runcie-Campbell angrily challenges them in the beach hut.

Calum in the world

Calum's good nature is his downfall. Neil protects him from the harsh realities of life but he is unable to protect him from Duror's unreasoning hatred. Duror's particular spite for Calum may have arisen because of Calum's lack of bitterness in the face of terrible physical disability. Calum accepts his lot without complaint and seems happy with the simplest things in life, whereas Duror, who has far more than Calum and Neil, is resentful of Peggy's disability and is tormented by his frustrated life.

It is interesting to note the contrast between Calum's affinity with nature and the destruction that Duror represents in his role as gamekeeper. At no place is this made more apparent than during the deer drive, an event that epitomises humanity's thoughtless destruction of nature. Lady Runcie-Campbell recognises the beauty of the deer but seems happy to kill them for sport, regarding them as her property. Captain Forgan comments on the strangeness of his hopes for a kill set alongside his departure for the North African front – a place where thousands of soldiers are being killed and where he will undoubtedly have to witness great slaughter. Yet Calum, on seeing the wounded deer, cannot set aside his empathy with nature. Again, Jenkins conveys Calum's innocence by linking him to the natural world as Calum 'too was a deer hunted by remorseless men'. The uncaring excitement of the hunters and Duror's savagery in cutting the deer's throat are set against Calum's desperate attempts to comfort the wounded deer, and Jenkins uses this characterisation to show Calum's innocent and pure nature.

The broken doll is also used to underline Calum's purity: in his hands it is an object from childhood to be treasured and repaired, a gift that can be returned to the family. However, in Duror's hands it becomes a corrupted and obscene thing, an object associated with loss of innocence and adult desires. Tulloch, another representative of goodness in the novel, recognises Calum's innocent reasons for taking the doll, but is astute enough to spot Duror's disturbing obsession with it and understands Lady Runcie-Campbell's alarm.

Although Calum would not survive without Neil to care for him, his innocent nature does provide a blanket against the harshness of the world the brothers inhabit. While Neil is caught up in thoughts of war, missed opportunities and the daily fight for survival, Calum is oblivious to these things. When the brothers start their journey to Lendrick, Neil worries about missing the bus and feels resentful over the Runcie-Campbells' cars, but Calum is happy to wait patiently on the fence and think of the pipe he will buy for Neil. Similarly, Calum's good nature means that he is opposed to them going to the beach hut: Neil's insistence that they shelter there indirectly contributes to Calum's death. Calum's lack of awareness of social class means that he is able to answer Lady Runcie-Campbell when Neil is socially embarrassed by her. However, her perception of Calum is based on his physical appearance, so she fails to see the goodness within him. The fact that he does not adhere to the code of social behaviour by having the temerity to answer her after he and Neil have 'invaded' her beach hut leads to her disliking the brothers even more.

His sacrifice

Calum's death is **foreshadowed** throughout the novel: the parallels with Christ, Duror and Neil's comments on sacrifice and Calum's remoteness from the real world all point to his inevitable death at Duror's hands. The description of his death presents him as a Christ-like figure: he dangles from the tree, his arms seeming to gesture in prayer as his blood drips to the ground with the cones he loves. In giving us this picture, Jenkins seems to be suggesting that Calum's death, like Christ's, has brought redemption and hope from the darkness that enveloped the woods.

Neil

Neil is the elder of the two McPhie brothers. He has taken on the responsibility of looking after Calum from a young age, setting aside his own ambitions of going to sea and marrying. Unlike Calum, he is acutely aware of the cruelties of life and is deeply resentful of the social inequalities created by the class system in Britain at that time. Yet, for all of Neil's bitterness, he has a good heart and cares deeply for his brother. Even when annoyed at Calum's simplistic view of events, he tries to exercise patience and apologises when he fails to do so. When in the treetops before the storm, for example, Neil finds it difficult to cope with Calum's excitement and talk of their dead mother in heaven, he is still able to tell Calum '…don't change. Keep being yourself. You're better than all of us' as they run towards the shelter of the beach hut.

Neil's resilient and practical nature contrasts with Calum's dreaminess and sensitivity, and while Calum is capable of living only in the present, Neil constantly worries about the future and who will look after Calum. Yet Neil's determination to stand up for equality and his refusal to help Roderick is an integral part of the events leading to Calum's death: Graham returns to pass on Neil's refusal to Lady Runcie-Campbell, meeting the suicidal Duror and thus inadvertently sealing their fate.

Key quotation

Neil (speaking to Calum): 'Is to be always happy a crime? Is it daft never to be angry or jealous or full of spite? You're better and wiser than any of them.'

Glossary

foreshadow: a literary technique in which a writer hints at future events in the story.

In many ways, Neil is a product of the world surrounding him – a hostile world, full of inequalities and suffering. In Lendrick, he and Calum are accepted and liked by the locals but there is the inevitable country gossip about the brothers' origins. The local men discuss the brothers' different fathers and the fact that their mother may have taken her own life after seeing Calum's disabilities. Neil is determined to fit into this small community – in the village, his grudging treatment of the conscientious objectors with whom he is normally friendly is evidence that he feels the need to conform to community behaviour.

Interestingly for a man who is so committed to the principles of social equality and justice, Neil is powerless in his dealings with the upper-class Lady Runcie-Campbell. Before being ejected from the beach hut, he protests to an unhappy Calum that they have every right to be in the hut, but when confronted by Lady Runcie-Campbell he cannot speak and cannot even meet her gaze. When the brothers pass the estate's car in Lendrick and Roderick greets them, we are told that Neil 'crumbled into the abjectness of a peasant', 'fumbled at his cap' and 'hurried away, not waiting for Calum'. For Neil, it is important that the social order changes so that ordinary people like him and Calum have a better life. As he does not believe in God, Neil hopes for equality but finds it difficult to make a stand in the face of the established power of the aristocracy. When he does stand up to Lady Runcie-Campbell's power – pushed beyond endurance by the deer hunt and her cold-hearted treatment in the beach hut – the eventual result is the death of Calum.

In some ways, Neil is a more tragic figure than Calum. He clearly loves his brother and seems to have lost everything at the end of the novel. His frantic attempts to reach his murdered brother indicate the depth of his loss and leave us feeling great sympathy for his desperate situation.

Lady Runcie-Campbell

Conflict between class and Christianity

Lady Runcie-Campbell is caught between the opposing ideals of Christianity and the expectations of a rigid class system. As the wife of Sir Colin Runcie-Campbell, she is expected to manage the estate while he serves in wartime and it is clear that she is quite capable of doing this. It is the arrival of the cone-gatherers and Duror's subsequent deterioration that provoke a conflict within her character.

Like Neil, she is a product of the society in which she lives: she is an aristocrat who, while still valuing all human beings, believes in her own superiority as a member of the upper class. Although it would be easy to condemn her for her poor treatment of the cone-gatherers, it is important to remember that she consults Duror at moments of crisis – fooled by

Build critical skills

Look at the dialogue between Neil and Calum during the storm and their arrival in the beach hut (Chapter 11). What do we learn about the relationship between the brothers?

his previous endurance and calm manner – and therefore does not gain a correct picture of events on her estate. In the absence of her husband, she finds herself trying to uphold a social order at odds with her own Christian beliefs.

Her relationship with her children shows her to be a caring mother. She is loving to both Sheila and Roderick, but is particularly worried about Roderick's health and future – especially as the future of the estate will rest with him. She is aware that her son has been influenced by her own father's thoughts on social equality and justice. Indeed, at some points in the novel, it is clear that she has been influenced by her father's compassion. For example, when she wishes to distance herself from Duror's predicament, she thinks of her father, a judge, having to sentence a murderer to death. She remembers her father agreeing with her own thoughts on the terrible implications of pronouncing such a terrible judicial sentence yet being aware that all human beings are connected to each other.

This sense of justice is shown when she decides to let the cone-gatherers remain on the estate despite Calum's actions during the deer hunt. Although she wishes them removed, she is willing to listen to Roderick and her brother making a case for Neil and Calum's continued employment on the estate. Perhaps Duror's voice would have had the opposite result, but Duror is unable to speak at this point so cannot influence her decision. It is also worth remembering that she is unaware of the true nature of the cone-gatherers' miserable hut and that it is Duror who has convinced her that they should not be allowed to use the beach hut for their accommodation.

The conflicting sides of her character are seen when she pays a visit to Peggy. Here, she struggles with her Christian duty. She is appalled by Peggy's fawning attention to her as a member of the upper class but feels that it is her duty as the laird's wife to visit a disabled tenant. Nevertheless, she also uses the visit as a way to atone for her refusal to listen to Roderick's request to give the cone-gatherers a lift home: looked at in this light, her visit is not without self-interest.

Her relationship with Duror

Her interaction with Duror reveals a weakness in her character. As his employer – and as someone who wishes to emulate Christ's compassion – she is possibly the only person who could prevent Duror's final acts. However, she chooses to ignore the signs that Duror is losing his grip on sanity. She is fully aware of his unhappy domestic circumstances; she herself admires the 'marvellous restraint' he shows during her visits to Peggy, yet she simply overlooks his increasingly dishevelled appearance, telling herself that he is merely tired. When Mrs Lochie shares her worries about Duror's increasingly bizarre behaviour, Lady Runcie-Campbell again

Key quotation

Lady Runcie-Campbell: 'To obey Christ by being humble must mean to betray her husband, and also, perhaps, to amuse her equals.'

ignores this plea for help, convincing herself that it is not her business. She has a further opportunity to prevent the final tragedy when an almost incoherent Duror delivers his bizarre and offensive story of Calum and the doll. Yet, even then, she chooses to be offended at his behaviour towards her rank rather than being concerned for his welfare. She demands that he is silent but then ironically asks, 'Have you gone mad? Do you realise whom you're talking to?'

Redemption

She is the last character we see in the novel, and her reaction to Calum's death and Duror's suicide could be interpreted in different ways. Why does she suddenly ask Baird to help Neil, and why does she drop to her knees and weep beside Calum's spilled blood and cones? Up until those points, she has treated the cone-gatherers badly. Are the hope and joy she feels caused by the news of Roderick's rescue or has Calum's death resolved the conflict within her? Perhaps the answer lies in Jenkins' mention of the single thought that dominates her mind throughout her desperate journey to find the cone-gatherers: she thinks regretfully of her expulsion of the cone-gatherers from the beach hut and she also seems to be in search of some kind of resolution 'without which she could never return'. Her compassion for Neil, her weeping and feelings of 'purified hope' suggest that these deaths offer a redemption from the evil that has dominated the woods.

Roderick Runcie-Campbell

▲ Roderick climbs to the dizzying heights of a silver fir tree, intent on gathering the precious cones

---

Build critical skills

Lady Runcie-Campbell's thoughts reveal some important facts about her husband, Sir Colin Runcie-Campbell. Make a note of everything we learn about his character.

Roderick is the elder child of Sir Colin and Lady Runcie-Campbell and is the heir to the Lendrickmore estate and the title. Unlike his younger sister Sheila, Roderick is uncomfortable with the societal expectations placed upon him. He seems unable to adopt the haughty attitude that Sir Colin feels is essential in ensuring that 'the lower orders' are kept in their rightful place. Roderick's kindness and strong sense of fairness are seen in his friendliness to the cone-gatherers: he defends them after the deer hunt and beach hunt incidents, he asks his mother to give them a lift and he tries to take the cake to them as an apology.

Lady Runcie-Campbell is reluctant to condemn this attitude as she realises that Roderick's compassion is commendable and was the reason for the special bond formed between Roderick and her father, the judge. Sir Colin, however, is angered by his son's attitude, believing that Roderick's equal treatment of everyone is an abandonment of his natural duties as an aristocrat.

It is clear that Roderick is an imaginative boy who, like Calum and Tulloch, symbolises goodness in the novel – certainly, he seems to harbour a distrust of Duror, whose character undoubtedly symbolises evil. His admiration of the cone-gatherers may be a result of his own self-sacrificing and contented nature: he sees the simplicity of the brothers' lives and instinctively recognises Calum's inner goodness. When he tries to visit Neil and Calum at their hut, he imagines himself in the footsteps of Christian heroes: Christian from Bunyan's *The Pilgrim's Progress* and Sir Galahad from the Arthurian legends. This not only shows his determination to correct the injustice of the deer drive but also reveals his naivety in imagining the brothers will be comfortable in the presence of a baronet's son.

Like Neil, Roderick is another character whose good deeds only bring tragedy. He climbs the tree, possibly copying the men he so admires, but it is more likely that he wishes to gather the forbidden silver fir cones as a gift for Calum and Neil. When his mother speaks to him on the morning of the tragedy, he clearly has a secret plan in mind, and his questioning of Tulloch suggests that he is aware of different species of trees. He also tells Tulloch that he wishes to say goodbye to the men, so it seems likely that he intends to give the cones to the men as a farewell gift. Again, there is a deep sense of irony in the fact that Roderick's determination to treat the brothers as equals fulfils Sir Colin's predictions of disaster.

Roderick's rescue from the tree by Harry, the humble gardening apprentice, suggests that there is hope for the future and that the social hierarchy will not remain so regimented. Roderick chooses Harry to accompany him on his unsuccessful attempt to take the cake to the cone-gatherers, and although Harry is not actually present when Roderick calls to ask him to accompany him on this 'pilgrimage', it seems clear that there is a friendship between the boys. This makes Lady Runcie-Campbell's physical punishment of Harry – when he timidly suggests

Key quotation

Roderick/Lady Runcie-Campbell: 'Roderick was now stronger in body, keener in mind, and still with that simplicity in his soul which so often showed up the twisted doubts in hers.'

that Roderick may not be able to descend the tree because of a fear of heights – seem all the more cold-hearted and unfair. Harry's loyalty to Roderick and his endurance throughout the rescue vindicate Roderick's trust and friendship towards those of a different class and suggest that class distinctions are a destructive force.

Minor characters

Sheila Runcie-Campbell

Roderick's younger sister provides a stereotypical view of the aristocracy at that time. She is indulged and shows no concern for individuals who do not share her privileged background. Where Roderick is caring and compassionate, she is self-centred and thinks only of her own comfort. This contrast between the Runcie-Campbell children is seen clearly when Roderick asks his mother to give the cone-gatherers a lift in the car. Sheila is horrified at the thought of sharing the car with Neil and Calum, and when Roderick points out that even dogs are allowed in the car, she has no qualms about telling him that Monty, her dog, matters far more to her than the cone-gatherers do.

At several other places in the novel, we see Sheila's callous disregard for those less fortunate than herself. After her mother has sent the cone-gatherers from the beach hut, she openly mocks the holes in Calum's pullover and seems to take pleasure from Neil's shame. Her lack of concern for Neil and Calum's safety in the storm, and her sniggering at their discomfort in the hut, provide a clear impression of the negative effects that can result from holding rank and privilege.

Peggy Duror

The wife of John Duror, Peggy is a character who has suffered greatly in life. We learn that she was once able-bodied and beautiful, and that she and Duror were very much in love. Now, she is bed-ridden, having become paralysed after only two years of marriage. She and Duror have been married for 20 years and, in the 18 years following Peggy's accident, she has grown monstrously obese. Duror's intolerance of physical imperfections has led to him being repelled by his wife's condition. His intolerance manifests itself not only in his reluctance to spend time with Peggy but also in his disturbing nightmare of her being pecked to death by thrushes and in his thoughts of Peggy as he kills the deer during the deer drive.

In Chapter 2, we see Duror speak briefly with her, but it is clear that he is desperate to leave her presence and that he does not love her. Peggy still loves Duror, however, and wants him to spend some time with her. Duror's continued avoidance of his wife leads to her becoming tearful and petulant. She yearns for the happy early days of their marriage, speaking to him of a treasured autumn memory where he adorned her hair with red rowan berries, but a cold-hearted Duror instantly dismisses her fond recollection, telling her 'the rowans are just about past'. His comment, linking to winter's arrival, symbolises the death of their marriage and the coldness with which he now views his wife.

We are never told the cause of Peggy's paralysis explicitly, but Duror's fleeting thought on 'that incommunicable phantom, his son' suggests that she may have been paralysed during childbirth and that the infant did not survive. Peggy's love of children is also mentioned and she seems to regret the absence of a child in their life. Whatever the cause of her paralysis, it is clear that her physical condition has prevented Duror and his wife from having a normal marriage. The effects of Duror's sexual frustration and repression are raised by Dr Matheson when Duror visits him following the disastrous events of the deer hunt. However, Duror remains tight-lipped about his mistaking the deer for Peggy and the only advice the doctor can give him is to continue to endure as he has been doing.

Dr Matheson

The doctor, although seeming to be professionally competent, is hardly the best advert for a caring member of the medical profession. He seems more concerned with the lack of luxury foodstuffs and wartime rationing than the needs of his patients. We first meet the doctor when he gives a lift to Duror late at night after Duror's solitary observation of the cone-gatherers' hut. Despite his seeming obsession with food and drink – and his hints about venison – the doctor is aware that all is not well with the gamekeeper. He studies Duror's reactions carefully when asking after Peggy.

Later in the novel, when Duror goes to see him at Lady Runcie-Campbell's insistence, the doctor's selfishness is seen in his greedy delight at Duror's gift of venison. He broaches the subject of Duror's unhappy marriage and tells Duror of the problems that can arise from frustration and repressed desires, but is unable to offer any real help. His selfish nature is made clear when, after failing to help Duror, he then encourages him to drink too much whisky while he burdens Duror with the details of his own unhappy domestic situation.

Tulloch

Tulloch is the head forester at Ardmore, and he is sympathetic to Neil and Calum's difficult lives. He does what he can to help them and is kind and respectful to all of the characters he meets. Neil turns to Tulloch for help after the brothers are ejected from the beach hut, suggesting that Neil sees him as a beacon of hope in an otherwise cruel and indifferent world. The brothers have spent five happy years at Ardmore, working under Tulloch's direction.

Key quotation

Dr Matheson (thinking of Duror): 'Yes, thought the doctor, poor Duror for all his pretence of self-possession and invulnerability had been fighting his own war for years: there must be deep wounds though they did not show...'

Build critical skills

The doctor's comments reveal some details of conditions at home during the Second World War. What do we learn from him?

Tulloch's good nature is seen in various places throughout the novel. He tries to warn Lady Runcie-Campbell about Calum's aversion to hunting, but is outmanoeuvred by Duror's scheming; he speaks up for Calum at the deer hunt and after the storm; he decently and discreetly rescues Lady Runcie-Campbell from a distressing situation by suggesting that the broken doll would suit his daughter; and he offers friendship and comfort to the brothers when he moves them to the sunnier Scour Point.

Tulloch's goodness is all the more surprising when we learn that – like Duror, Neil and Calum – he has experienced hatred and difficult circumstances. We are told that he has been ridiculed for his slightly unusual looks, but his strength of character is such that he is able to laugh off these insults. He is able to reflect humorously on his wife's retaliation to those who still make jokes about his appearance. We also see that he avoids hurting others even when he is subject to injustice. He is willing to help the conscientious objectors and bears an unfair and hurtful rebuke from Lady Runcie-Campbell when he could easily have pointed out his own losses. His compassion for others allows him to think carefully before he acts and avoid causing unnecessary pain. His young family are a source of great joy to him.

Mrs Lochie

Peggy's mother, Mrs Lochie, is a devout character who raises questions about how far religion can offer comfort. She keeps house for Duror and Peggy but finds this a difficult burden as she grows older. She is willing to slander Duror to all who will listen, suggesting that she does not like her son-in-law – possibly because of his cold treatment towards her daughter. Mrs Lochie seems an embittered woman who is unhappy at the way her own and her daughter's lives have become dull and lacking in hope. She is probably one of the reasons why Duror spends so much time outside his home.

Mrs Morton

As the widowed cook/housekeeper for the Runcie-Campbell family, Mrs Morton seems to be a sensible and kind person. She secretly has hopes of marrying Duror should anything happen to his wife. Her fondness for Duror is used by him when he lies about Calum committing indecent acts in the woods; he hopes she will spread this rumour. Her common sense means that she is initially reluctant to believe him, but she does pass on his lies when Lady Runcie-Campbell asks her about Duror's increasingly erratic behaviour.

Her caring nature is shown in her ready provision of the cake which Roderick requests. She is kind to him, and he treats her respectfully in return, asking after her son who is serving in the merchant navy. It is Mrs Morton who brings news of Roderick's plight in the silver fir and her concern for Roderick's safety is genuine. Duror recognises her goodness and briefly considers the hope she could bring but he rejects this opportunity in favour of his dark plans for the cone-gatherers' destruction.

Captain Forgan

Lady Runcie-Campbell's brother is present on two occasions during the novel. He plays cricket on the lawn with Roderick and Sheila, and he is present at the deer drive arranged in his honour. Both of these activities are closely associated with the upper-class society of which he is a member. His upper-class origins are suggested by the public schoolboyish manner of speech we see in his conversation with Duror. He seems to be a considerate and good man who is sensitive enough to admit to Duror that he will treasure his memories of Lendrickmore when on active service. His good nature is also apparent in his happy dealings with the children and when he tells his sister that he bears no ill will to the cone-gatherers after the deer drive has been disrupted.

Household staff

Although the war would have caused a drastic reduction in the number of servants available for work on country estates, it is likely that we have not met all of the Runcie-Campbells' staff in this novel. However, the inclusion of Harry, Erchie, Manson, Baird, Jean (the maid) and Charlie is representative of the outdoor and indoor staff who would have served a titled family of that time – Duror and Mrs Morton are more important in the hierarchy of servants. Betty the land girl adds humour and reinforces the story's wartime setting. The inclusion of these characters who serve the estate in a variety of different roles also enhances our understanding of Lady Runcie-Campbell's elevated position in society and the great responsibility she holds in managing the estate in Sir Colin's absence.

REVIEW YOUR LEARNING

(Answers are given on p. 109.)

1 What is the name of the Runcie-Campbells' housekeeper?
2 What was Lady Runcie-Campbell's father's occupation?
3 Why is Sir Colin concerned about his son, Roderick?
4 Who looks after Duror's wife, Peggy?
5 What symbol is often used by Jenkins when describing the deterioration in Duror's mental state?
6 What occupation did Neil forsake to look after Calum?
7 Who says, 'After this war, the lower orders are going to be frightfully presumptuous'?

3.3 Themes

Target your thinking

- What does 'theme' mean?
- What are the main themes in *The Cone-Gatherers*?
- How does Jenkins use symbolism to convey themes?
- How are the setting, characters and events used to convey the novel's themes?

What does 'theme' mean?

To fully appreciate any literary work, it is important that you understand what is meant by 'theme'. If you understand this important aspect of the text, you will gain far more from your study of it – and you will be able to discuss theme with confidence in your exam answers.

What does theme mean? Put simply, it means the central idea(s) explored within a text. Theme, therefore, is not a literary technique: instead, it is an integral part of a literary work, an idea that the writer wants us to consider. A writer may be interested in an idea or an issue and may then choose to explore that idea or issue by creating a text based around it. Features such as characterisation, plot, setting, symbolism and language techniques can then be used by the writer to encourage readers to think about that idea. In summary, a theme is an idea that the writer wants us to think about when we are reading the text – and possibly long after we have finished reading.

Many works of literature have more than one theme. In *The Cone-Gatherers*, Jenkins explores several themes. As you read the text, you will certainly find yourself wondering why characters act in a certain way or what will happen after a key incident: whenever you do this, you will also be thinking about some of the themes that are a central part of the novel.

Thinking about the main themes can be a useful way to revise the novel after you have become familiar with the plot and characters. As already noted, several themes are explored in *The Cone-Gatherers* and there is some overlap between these themes. The main themes are as follows:

- good and evil – and the conflict between them
- social class
- war
- nature
- religion

Good and evil

The battle between good and evil has been a theme in literature since the dawn of time: even before the written word, humanity has been fascinated with questions of right and wrong and what makes us commit evil deeds or stand on the side of goodness. It is hardly surprising, therefore, that Jenkins also chooses to consider these 'big' questions.

It is important to remember that the novel was written in the aftermath of the Second World War and published in 1955. This was a time when many people would still have been reflecting on the horrors of the war and there would have been discussion of why these terrible evils had taken place. Other people's experiences and thoughts on the war would have influenced Jenkins' writing and the novel's development: at several points in the novel, characters mention atrocities being committed as the war is fought in Europe and beyond, and several characters discuss why these terrible events are happening.

Another influence on *The Cone-Gatherers* would have been the strong tradition of Scottish works of literature dealing with good and evil in the lives of everyday men and women. As a Scottish writer who had gained a degree in English at the University of Glasgow, Jenkins would have been well acquainted with the works of Robert Burns, James Hogg, Robert Louis Stevenson and other Scottish writers whose works often explored humanity's struggle with good and evil.

The characters of Duror and Calum are on opposite sides in the battle between light and darkness, good and evil. In the Characterisation section of this guide, Duror and Calum's symbolic functions within this conflict are noted: Duror becomes a symbol of evil and Calum represents goodness. Although Calum is too simple a man to be aware of his role in this struggle, Duror consciously aligns himself with evil.

It is worth considering in more detail how each of these characters is used by Jenkins to explore the themes of good and evil, and the ongoing battle between these forces.

Good

Although there are several good characters in the novel, it is the unwitting Calum who becomes the oppositional force to Duror's evil and who symbolises good. Calum is a truly good character – at no point in the novel does he commit any act which could be viewed as cruel or harmful to others. He is accepting of his disability and seems happy with the simple life he and Neil lead. We never see Calum complain about any aspect of the brothers' difficult lives and, when viewed alongside Duror's pent-up frustration and rage, it is clear that Calum's simple joy in life is a clear sign of his goodness.

This is highlighted in his compassion for all creatures – including people – and in his innocent enjoyment of nature. We first meet Calum at home in the trees where he is closely associated with the gentler creatures of the natural world. Jenkins describes him as being 'as indigenous as a squirrel' and the chaffinches which surround him are said to be 'his friends', suggesting that he is at one with nature and that animals sense no threat in him. Calum's climbing ability and his ease in the highest branches of the trees could also symbolise his nearness to God: unlike his brother Neil, he believes in God and has a childlike view of heaven.

Calum has no understanding of cruelty and becomes deeply distressed by the suffering of others. Neil and Tulloch are also good men, but they carry the normal burdens of life in their hearts and have had to make compromises in order to live. Calum's purity and detachment from worldly concerns keep him in a childhood state of innocence. Even his hobby of carving animals from the pieces of dead wood that he finds on the forest floor suggests he has an ability to resurrect beauty and joy, and to bring warmth to others. Duror is envious of this ability: he sees himself as being like a dying tree, with no hope of resurrection, so perhaps he recognises that Calum possesses a precious quality and inner beauty that he will never have. We also learn that Tulloch's young daughter cherishes a wooden squirrel that Calum has carved for her. Again, this links Calum with the childlike qualities of innocence and purity. This is in direct opposition to Duror, who has no childlike qualities.

Evil

Duror is the **antagonist** of the novel. He sets out to rid the woods of Calum, despite knowing that Calum has done no harm and is an innocent. Disillusioned with his own life, Duror eventually believes that destroying Calum will end his own torment and restore his sanity. He deliberately sets out to harm Calum in several ways: he spreads lies that could destroy the brothers' lives; he manipulates events so that Calum is forced to participate in a hunt where he could easily be killed because of his concern for animals; and he falsely accuses the pure and innocent Calum of abusing Sheila's doll.

Duror is often presented to us at night-time or lurking in the shadows of the woods. He is a threatening and malign presence. The lies he tells and his irrational hatred in the beautiful woods of Lendrickmore are a reflection of the serpent in the perfect Garden of Eden. According to several religious traditions, evil and sin first entered the world when Satan, disguised as a serpent, tempted the first humans, Adam and Eve, to eat fruit from the tree of knowledge. Satan, the devil, is also known as 'the father of lies' and is the embodiment of evil in several religions. Duror's scheming and lying, and his presence in a place of beauty such

Key quotation

Calum: 'This was the terrifying mystery, why creatures he loved should kill one another.'

Glossary

antagonist: in literature, a person or force that is set against the story's protagonist (often seen as the 'main' character or hero). An antagonist often acts in a hostile or immoral manner.

as the woods, makes it clear to us that he is an evil character. Like Satan, Duror is fuelled by envy and rage, and he brings destruction to the Eden-like woods. Roderick recognises Duror as the personification of evil when he sees him lurking outside the brothers' hut.

Near the end of the novel, Duror seems to have been completely overtaken by evil. When he is ordered to hand over the doll to a distressed Lady Runcie-Campbell, she senses the evil within him and almost seems afraid she will be infected by it. She holds the doll 'as if it was visibly soiling her hand' and is glad of Tulloch's reassuring presence.

Jenkins also seems to be suggesting that we have the power to choose between good and evil. Although Duror has had to face difficulties in his life, the same can be said of many other characters in the novel. However, unlike the other characters, Duror chooses an evil path through life's hardships. His dark path leads him into greater evil, the climax of which is murder and suicide. Calum's murder and Duror's suicide are foreshadowed throughout the novel, leading to a sense of inevitability surrounding the final tragedy. Jenkins uses the religious idea of sacrifice in relation to Calum's fate, ensuring that we see Duror as totally evil. In the Bible's presentation of Christ's sacrifice, Jesus is betrayed by his disciple Judas Iscariot and Judas hangs himself after learning that Christ will be crucified. Duror's suicide after the murder of the innocent Calum is a clear parallel to the Bible's story of Judas's betrayal. Just as Judas Iscariot's name has become synonymous with evil and betrayal, so too is Duror's character strongly associated with evil.

Yet Duror's suicide and Lady Runcie-Campbell's renewed hope as she weeps beside the murdered Calum show that evil does not win in this conflict. We are left with the idea that Calum's death has been a sacrifice that has brought redemption and that goodness can banish evil. It is therefore important to consider how Jenkins conveys the theme of good and how it can triumph over evil.

The conflict between good and evil

Although good and evil can be viewed as individual themes in the novel, there is an obvious overlap of these ideas and the struggle between these opposing forces is presented in a variety of ways. Most notably, this conflict is explored through the characterisation of Duror and Calum. It is also explored through Jenkins' presentation of key incidents such as the deer hunt and the climax of Calum's murder; the novel's different settings; and the events that take place in the wartime world outside Lendrickmore.

We can see that Calum and Duror are characterised as direct opposites and Jenkins uses **contrast** to convey the struggle between the two forces they represent. Outwardly, Calum is deformed, but he has an inner

Key quotation

Roderick, on seeing Duror in the woods: '...he would never have noticed the lurker under the cypress, entangled in the thin green bony arms that curled out like an octopus's. No sunshine struck there, and even the luminance from the hut seemed to fail... Here at the very hut was the most evil presence of all, and it was visible.'

Glossary

contrast: the difference(s) between two things. In literature, contrast is often used to show divisions between people or ideas.

Key quotation

Duror: 'He was like a tree still straight, still showing green leaves; but underground death was creeping along the roots.'

Build critical skills

The deer hunt and Calum's murder are important incidents in the novel's exploration of the battle between good and evil, but there are others. Make a note of any other events that convey this conflict.

beauty and a good soul. Duror is the exact reverse of this: he is physically attractive – although his physical condition declines in tandem with his mental deterioration – but inwardly is tormented and devoid of all good feelings. We see Calum at home in the trees and creating wooden carvings that seem to come to life in his crippled hands; in contrast, we see Duror clumsy and almost paralysed by fear when he climbs the tree and the symbol of a dying tree is used to portray Duror's deterioration. The contrast between the characters is clear and we quickly realise that they stand on either side of this immense conflict.

Key events also show the conflict between good and evil. In the deer drive, Calum's concern for the wounded deer shows his willingness to sacrifice his own safety for another creature. This is in contrast to Duror's savagery, as he reacts with 'furious force' and is described as cutting the deer's throat 'savagely'. In that same chapter (Chapter 6), the failure of Duror's plan for the removal of the brothers is used by Jenkins to introduce the ideas of sacrifice and crucifixion. As Lady Runcie-Campbell and the other participants in the deer drive discuss whether Calum and Neil will be sent back to Ardmore, Duror fears that Calum will 'live happily' there and that this will only increase his own torment. At that point, he comes to believe that his only hope lies in the sacrifice of Calum, which he believes 'must be a destruction, an agony, a crucifixion'. In the climax of the novel, the symbolism of the crucifixion is then used to emphasise the resolution of the conflict between good and evil. Like Christ on the cross, Calum hangs from the tree and his death, along with the death of evil through Duror's suicide, is the sacrifice that brings Lady Runcie-Campbell renewed hope for a better life.

Settings are also used to convey the themes of good and evil. Setting the novel in a time of war allows Jenkins to explore the idea of evil committed under the guise of national interest. Several of the characters struggle with pain and grief at the loss of loved ones: Tulloch has lost a much-loved brother and Neil recalls some of the terrible things that are taking place in the war. We see Duror, a character steeped in evil, secretly approving the Nazis' use of concentration camps.

It is not only the setting in time which allows these themes to be conveyed. The estate is also a setting that can suggest both themes. Scour Point, for example, is described as 'the most beautiful place on the estate', yet it is the place where Calum is murdered and Duror takes his own life. The placing of the terrible final events in such a beautiful setting allows Jenkins to suggest that evil can exist in the least expected places. When Duror watches the cone-gatherers in their hut, he stands in the dark shadow of a cypress – a tree associated with mourning and commonly planted in cemeteries. By linking Duror with this setting, Jenkins is perhaps hinting that evil brings no light and we can never flourish in its shadow; it can bring only death. Calum, however, is associated with the pines, larches and firs where he gathers the cones in sunlight. The cones falling from his bag in the final scene suggest that, even in death, goodness creates promise for the future.

Social class

The social hierarchy

Issues surrounding social-class **structures and hierarchies** are explored throughout the novel, and the characters can be assigned to the social classes that were an important aspect of society at that time. We see the hierarchy of social class in action on the Lendrickmore estate, where the upper-class Runcie-Campbell family are served by the lower-class staff. All of the servants would be regarded as working class; this tier of the class system would also include Duror, Mrs Morton, Mr Baird and Tulloch who, although having more responsible jobs, are still regarded as coming from the lower orders of society. As impoverished forestry workers, Calum and Neil would be regarded as being at the lower end of the working class. The middle class is represented by Dr Matheson.

structures and hierarchies: in wartime Britain – and to an even greater degree before the war – many aspects of British society were based around a class system in which everyone knew their place and kept to it.

The aristocracy

Members of the aristocracy at the upper end of the class hierarchy, exemplified in the novel by Sir Colin and Lady Runcie-Campbell, are shown as being opposed to any breakdown of the strict class system that existed at that time. Although Sir Colin is not directly seen in the novel, Jenkins gives us a clear idea of his views by showing us Lady Runcie-Campbell's thoughts on her husband and the management of the estate and its people.

Sir Colin is the laird of his estate: he has a title and his family have owned the land for generations. His position in society is a privileged one and it is clear that he views himself and his family as being superior to those of lesser rank. Several times, Lady Runcie-Campbell reflects on Sir Colin's disapproval of Roderick's far less rigid attitude to the classes. She remembers that her husband believes in rank on Earth and in heaven, and that he is unwilling to behave in any way that goes against that strict class order; he even believes that the clergy are subject to his natural superiority, telling her that the minister must 'be treated with that correct degree of condescension which was never offensive but which indubitably was the true preserver of society'. In a time when many people looked up to the clergy as representing God's power on Earth, Sir Colin's perception of his own superior and separate status is a clear indicator that he places more faith in class boundaries than in any higher spiritual power.

Sheila has similar views to her father, openly admitting that she has no concern for those of a lower class. For Sheila, her dog is more important

Key quotation

Sir Colin Runcie-Campbell, speaking of the lower classes to his wife: 'They're still brutes under the skin, y'know. It's taken centuries of breeding to produce our kind. For God's sake don't get us mixed.'

than those who serve her or her family and she accepts her privileged background as something that is rightfully hers on account of her high-born position in society.

Roderick, however, seems to have quite different views from those of his sister. We learn that Sir Colin is deeply concerned about Roderick's compassion for those of a lower class and that he repeatedly condemns Roderick's 'friendliness towards inferiors' in the letters he sends to his wife. Roderick's tutor, Mr Sorn-Wilson, has also 'warned' Lady Runcie-Campbell about her son's kind treatment of servants and those of the lower classes. We see Roderick showing concern for the cone-gatherers and sensitively asking for Mrs Morton's son – something his father would almost certainly never consider doing. Jenkins depicts Roderick – a young character with imagination, humanity and vision – as representing a more hopeful future. Roderick has inherited his mother's and grandfather's Christian compassion but, unlike his forebears, he is not so rigidly steeped in the oppressive system of class. In fact, it is Roderick's decision to gather cones in the silver fir that eventually leads to the renewal of hope and the destruction of evil. Perhaps Jenkins is suggesting that the younger generation, as embodied in Roderick, have the power to eradicate class discrimination and bring a brighter future.

In contrast with Roderick's clear-sighted vision of a fairer and more equal world, Lady Runcie-Campbell struggles with the conflict between her social rank and her Christian ideals. She wishes to show Christian compassion, but is restricted by society's ideas on how a woman of her class should behave. At times, this conflict between social class and Christian values makes her a weak character. When Roderick wishes to give the cone-gatherers a lift, she instinctively refuses and thinks that Roderick's suggestion is 'absurd'; yet she also feels sorry for Calum and Neil. Torn between these conflicting ideals, she makes the error of turning to Duror for advice and this allows him to commence his lies about Calum. He hints that he knows something bad about Calum and then tells her 'the little one is an evil person'.

Lady Runcie-Campbell's arrogance is made apparent in her adoption of upper-class superiority at several points in the story, and this helps to convey that a rigid class system is unfeeling and destructive. After ordering Neil and Calum from the beach hut, she cannot understand Roderick's distress and is willing to listen to Sheila's cruel mockery of Neil and Calum. Although she does listen to Tulloch's defence of the brothers before the deer drive and when she wishes to send them from the estate, she always puts the interests of her position as a baronet's wife before her Christianity. Consequently, she is willing to order the men to take part in the deer hunt and to rescue Roderick from the tree – despite the fact that they are not her servants. The only time we see her abandon her superior manner is when she races to ask for the brothers' help after they have refused unless she asks them herself. However, her decision to go to them is almost certainly a result of her natural desire to protect Roderick rather than a sudden admission of the cone-gatherers' possession of equal humanity. Even after Calum's death, it is unclear whether she is fully aware of her role in the tragedy, although her tears and 'pity' suggest she feels some regret for what has happened. Her internal struggle conveys the idea that a rigid social class structure is completely at odds with equality and Christian compassion.

Key quotation

Lady Runcie-Campbell: 'Your father's right. After this war, the lower orders are going to be frightfully presumptuous.'

Working-class life

If the Runcie-Campbells provide us with a picture of upper-class attitudes, almost all of the other characters show the restrictive nature of working-class life. Neil is perhaps the best example of a character whose life has been hemmed in by his social class. Although his life is undeniably restricted by having to care for Calum – he abandoned his dreams of going to sea and marrying to care for his brother – he does not resent the limitations this brings. He does, however, resent the inequalities created by the class system. When we first see Neil, he is gazing at the great house with 'bitter intentness' and comparing the upper-class luxury of the Runcie-Campbells' house with the hut he and Calum share. He comments on injustice and inequality at various points in the novel, bemoaning the poverty of the brothers' living conditions or worrying about being completely at Lady Runcie-Campbell's mercy with regards to their employment.

Jenkins suggests the restrictive power of class division when Neil, a proponent of equal rights, remains submissive in his encounters with Lady Runcie-Campbell. He is unable to answer her when she demands an explanation for his presence in the beach hut, despite previously telling Calum that they have a 'right to be alive' and seek shelter. He is also unable to look her in the eye when passing the car in Lendrick; instead, he makes an almost feudal gesture of greeting and addresses Roderick as 'sir'. Neil is unable to throw off the conventions of a society ruled by class divisions. Yet, resentful though he is of her power and wealth, Neil does not understand that Lady Runcie-Campbell is also restricted by the class system. Tulloch sees the conflict taking place within Lady Runcie-Campbell and he tries to explain this to Neil. However, Neil is unable to see past the physical evidence of upper-class wealth and privilege, and – unaware of Duror's corruption of Lady Runcie-Campbell – believes that she lacks any feelings for the classes beneath her.

Although shocked at the horrors taking place in the war, Neil hopes that the sacrifices made will bring about a world in which the class system no longer matters. When speaking to Tulloch after the storm, Neil refers to

Key quotation

Neil, thinking of the war: '…the proud claims of honour and independence and courage made on behalf of his country at war affected him deeply in his own private attitude: it was necessary now for him to fight back against every injustice inflicted on him, and especially on his brother.'

the children who are innocent victims of war and the two men discuss how this may result in future generations being 'able to grow up and live like free men'. It is clear that Neil desperately wishes for a more equal world, and we learn that he believes the war is being fought for noble causes and that the class system will be destroyed.

▲ The cone-gatherers' hut was tiny and poorly constructed

While Neil shows one aspect of working-class views, the servants at Lendrickmore reveal a slightly different aspect. Many of them seem quite accepting of their place in the lower orders of society. Duror is described as having an 'aloof submissiveness' and Lady Runcie-Campbell places considerable value on this aspect of his character. We also learn that Peggy fawns upon her and feels honoured by a visit from a member of the aristocracy. Even when suffering injustice, the servants remain submissive throughout the novel: the elderly Erchie Graham carries out demanding physical tasks for his mistress and the far younger Harry does not react when Lady Runcie-Campbell physically assaults him. In the climax of the novel, Erchie Graham is aghast at Neil's refusal to help and his demand that the mistress of the estate comes to ask for his help in person. Erchie is impressed by Neil's stubbornness, but also shows his awareness of class conventions when he exclaims, 'The mistress! Are you daft!…You can't expect her to come like a byremaid and say "please!".'

When we consider the ways in which almost all of the characters conform to the expectations placed upon them by social class, the ending of the novel becomes even more powerful. Jenkins leaves us with the dramatic image of the aristocratic Lady Runcie-Campbell weeping and seemingly in an attitude of prayer below the humble cone-gatherer whose sacrificial blood falls to earth with the precious cones. Perhaps this reversal of the normal social order – with Lady Runcie-Campbell looking up to Calum instead of looking down on him – suggests she has suddenly become aware that her responsibilities as a Christian are more important than the responsibilities dictated by her class.

War

As we have seen, the time period in which *The Cone-Gatherers* is set allows Jenkins to explore the theme of social class, but the time setting of the Second World War allows him to consider the destructive nature of war. There is an overlap between these two themes: as we have seen, the novel considers the way in which the war changes attitudes to social class and class structure. However, Jenkins also considers the destructive nature of war: even small and remote communities such as Lendrickmore and Ardmore are negatively affected by the war being waged in the wider world.

The theme of war arises early in the novel; indeed, it is mentioned on the first page. Immediately after a description of the beautiful natural landscape comes a startling description of three aspects of war. A 'destroyer' represents the war being fought at sea, swooping fighter planes represent the battles being fought in the air and the crack of gunshots in the woods – although possibly only coming from a gamekeeper or poacher's gun – reminds us of the fighting on land. In this, the second paragraph of the novel, Jenkins suggests that war is all-encompassing. These presences on land, sea and air, and in a place so far removed from the front lines of the war, emphasise that war has the power to contaminate everything. Of course, the novel was written after the war and, as readers, we are likely to be aware of the war's history: the battles fought in countries, skies and seas across the world; the bombing and blitzes that caused widespread devastation in cities across Europe; the horrors of Hiroshima and Nagasaki. We know that military and civilian casualties were enormous. At the beginning of the novel Jenkins, a committed pacifist and a conscientious objector, gives us this depiction of the machinery of war in a beautiful place in order to remind us of the destructive and immoral aspects of war.

In several places, Neil comments on the human cost of war. When Calum is upset at the thought of the wood being cut down, Neil reminds him that 'there are more men than trees being cut down', and when Tulloch thinks of his brother killed at Dunkirk, we learn that the war has claimed victims even in this remote and peaceful place. Mrs Morton and Lady Runcie-Campbell are affected by thoughts of losing loved ones and it is made clear that the topic of war dominates everyone's life. Jenkins ensures that war is never a distant presence in this novel: it creeps into every aspect of life – Mrs Lochie listens to news of the war on the radio;

Duror reads a newspaper headline about the Battle of Stalingrad; and war is the dominant topic of discussion from hotel bar to doctor's surgery.

Of course, the war is also the reason for Neil and Calum's presence in the woods at Lendrickmore, as they collect the cones that will be used to re-establish the forests cut down for the war effort. Thus, it could be argued that Calum's death is ultimately caused by the war. It is true that the brothers' arrival in the woods is the catalyst for the final tragedy, but Duror's deteriorating mental health is also a result of his failure to be accepted for active service. Duror tells Captain Forgan that, despite being told that he is 'too old' for active service, he has tried to enlist three times and will try again. We also learn that he is bitterly envious of a younger man, John Farquharson, who is serving in the North African desert. Duror seems to be the only character who sees the war as something positive and this further emphasises his symbolic association with evil.

Jenkins also explores the theme of war's destructive influence by giving us an insight into the lives of the conscientious objectors who work with Tulloch. There is little doubt that Jenkins' own experiences as a conscientious objector can be seen in the novel. He participated in forestry work and cone-gathering in Argyll for his wartime service, and would undoubtedly have experienced negative attitudes similar to those demonstrated by the Lendrick villagers in his novel.

The conscientious objectors are badly treated by the local people when they arrive at Ardmore. Despite the fact that they are carrying out dangerous and essential work – and have to endure very basic accommodation – they are regarded as 'yellow-bellies' and shunned by the locals. The divisive nature of war is demonstrated by the fact that, initially, the conscientious objectors have to put up with open hostility from the estate workers and villagers alike. Only Calum and Tulloch treat them with kindness and friendship. Even Neil, who works alongside these men at Ardmore, is reluctant to speak with them in Lendrick, preferring to let the locals believe he shares their contempt for the newcomers. Yet, gradually, the Ardmore foresters come to accept the conscientious objectors as they get to know them. Neil reflects that this respect is because the incomers feel pride in their stance, believe that they have done no wrong and have no quarrel with the locals. Here, Jenkins emphasises the importance of following a moral code that urges respect for everyone rather than surrendering to the divisive hatred of war.

Nature

Jenkins explores differing aspects of nature throughout the novel, showing the natural world to be a dynamic and ever-changing force. One of the ways in which this theme is conveyed is through associating characters with different aspects of nature. Calum is the character who is most comfortable in the natural world. We have already seen that he is associated with the gentler creatures of the woods – squirrels, rabbits, deer and finches – but he is also aware of the more savage side of nature. He knows that animals have to kill each other to survive, and even imagines himself as an owl swooping down to the forest floor to catch prey, but he cannot understand this cruel and savage side of nature. He faces a similar predicament when he thinks of hunting and he is unable to understand why the hunters kill for sport. Calum cannot stand to watch suffering in other creatures, perhaps because of his empathy with everything in the natural world. This is one of the reasons why he is excused from the deer hunts at Ardmore. In the woods of Lendrickmore, however, his natural sensitivity is not viewed as sufficient reason to exclude him from the hunt.

Despite Calum's recognition of the cruelty of the natural world, he is attracted by its beauty – so much so that he becomes completely absorbed in it at times. He is completely at home in the trees and, even when on the ground, is preoccupied by his surroundings in the woods. Before the visit to Lendrick, he and Neil once again come across the deer in the forest and their contrasting reactions reveal a great deal about their characters. Calum is entranced and seems to belong with the herd of deer. But the deer are a painful reminder of the hunt for Neil, who angrily drives them away, revealing his lack of affinity with nature. This lack of understanding is further emphasised when Calum then tries to tell Neil he wished to apologise to the deer. A frustrated and mystified Neil tells Calum that humans cannot communicate with wild animals, yet Calum calmly insists that this is possible 'if you like them'. Calum's statement touches on the idea that innocence and respect for the natural world are essential qualities for those who wish to truly understand nature.

Neil respects nature, but he is often afraid of it. Unlike Calum, he is not entirely at home in the trees and he finds cone-gathering a difficult task. When Tulloch comes across Neil after the storm, he sees that the work in the woods has badly affected Neil's health and his arthritis has worsened. Calum seems to be unaffected by the storm, despite Neil's worries about his brother's chest problems. Thus, the storm is another part of the natural world that has differing aspects for the brothers. Neil regards the storm as a threatening and dangerous force, but Calum is excited by it and associates the strangely lit sky with the idea of a heavenly message. Neil's everyday worries and responsibilities distance him from the natural world so he fears it, but Calum's innocent acceptance of it means that he never sees nature as a truly hostile force.

Duror is also associated with the natural world, but in a very different way from Calum and Neil. As a gamekeeper, Duror sees his role as one in which nature must be controlled. He is most closely associated with his dogs – creatures that are domesticated rather than wild – so his link with nature is very different from that of the brothers. His attitude to the natural world is uneasy at times. He is most definitely not at home in the

Key quotation

Calum: 'This was the terrifying mystery, why creatures he loved should kill one another.'

trees, where he becomes dizzy and ashamed when he is unable to climb very high in his search for the cone-gatherers. His cruel treatment of the rabbits in the snares and his savage slaughter of the wounded deer reveal his desire to master living creatures rather than co-exist with them.

It is interesting that Jenkins frequently uses the symbolism of trees to describe Duror. On the surface, this would suggest that Duror is a part of nature, but we see that the tree within Duror is diseased and rotting, suggesting both that he is disconnected from the natural world and that his once 'stalwart' personality is gradually being eroded by mental illness. His violent nature and need for control are also conveyed when Jenkins describes his dark thoughts as being like 'a roaring, a storm through a tree'. Duror's lack of connection to the natural world is shown by the fact that he can no longer contemplate the elm that previously offered him comfort. Immediately after Calum's murder, Duror is described as a desolate character who has committed a terrible crime against nature. In doing so, he seems to have set aside his right to remain within the natural order of things. Only death can provide him with the relief that he can no longer find in nature.

Religion

Religion plays an important role in the lives of several of the novel's characters and, unsurprisingly, the theme of religion is closely linked to the twin themes of good and evil. Lady Runcie-Campbell is the character who is most affected by religious belief. She tries to follow Christian teachings in all aspects of her life, and genuinely attempts to show kindness and justice to others while preserving her status as a member of the gentry. We have already seen that this causes a conflict within her and that she is therefore sometimes unable to follow her religious ideals. Nevertheless, the workers on the estate view her as 'fair-minded'. Even Duror, who appears to have thought deeply on the nature of faith, associates her with religion and believes that she has 'an ability to exalt people out of their humdrum selves', suggesting that religion can be a force for good.

We see that Lady Runcie-Campbell often consults her faith for answers in times of crisis. When Tulloch telephones her to warn her of Calum's sensitivity to hunting, she initially wonders if Calum has 'some outlandish religious objection', but rejects this after reflecting on her own views as a 'reasonably conscientious Christian'. She has a narrow view of religion — she dismisses Roderick's mention of Buddha lightly — yet her faith also ensures her genuine concern for those in need. Her visits to Peggy and her doubts about her treatment of the cone-gatherers indicate that she has a conscience. It is unfortunate that, on several occasions, her awareness of her authority and social position takes precedence over the demands of her faith.

Build critical skills

Lady Runcie-Campbell and her son Roderick both show an appreciation for nature. Make a note of where their characters reflect on the beauty and/or power of the natural world.

Key quotation

Duror, thinking of the conflict within Lady Runcie-Campbell: 'He guessed that within her was a struggle between her Christian sympathy for the weak-minded hunchback and her pride as a patrician, to whom hunting on her own estate was as sacred as singing in church.'

Other characters are used to suggest that religion can be less helpful and is not always a comfort. Mary Black, the judgemental wife of the Lendrickmore forester, is one such example, as she cruelly tells Mrs Lochie that Peggy's fate is 'a punishment inflicted by God'. When Mrs Lochie questions her on how God could 'punish' Peggy in such a cruel way, she is given no satisfactory answer. When Duror mentions Peggy's 'reward' in heaven, she is disgusted at the seeming injustice of a tortured life rewarded by 'pampering the dead'. She tells Duror that she has her 'own religion', but she is still unable to explain the injustices that exist all around her. In a similar way, Mrs Morton, the kindly housekeeper, is conventionally religious but when speaking to Roderick is still unable to hide her doubts about God's caring nature.

Duror's attitude to religion is more ambiguous. His conversation with his mother-in-law reveals that he has thought deeply about faith and the notion of an afterlife, but when she asks him if he believes in a reward after death, he tells her that he does not. Nevertheless, he seems to be unsure of his answer, as he later mentions 'the other side' of the grave. He also believes that it is 'too late' for him to receive God's mercy and he feels a deep sense of loss. For Duror, it is clear that religion offers no hope.

On the other hand, Calum, whose delighted preoccupation with nature is reminiscent of religious faith, openly tells Neil that he believes in God and heaven. Just before the storm, he is excited by the light streaming down from the sky and asks Neil if it comes from heaven. He also tells Neil that he has seen their mother 'up there'. To the simple and accepting Calum, faith is comforting. Neil has no such faith and he tells Calum bleakly that heaven is 'just a name to please children'. The contrast between Calum's simple acceptance and Neil's cynical disbelief highlights the differing levels of faith seen in other characters.

REVIEW YOUR LEARNING

(Answers are given on p. 109.)

1 What is a theme?
2 What are the main themes in *The Cone-Gatherers*?
3 Name some of the techniques that Jenkins uses to convey the novel's themes.
4 What themes are explored through the characterisation of Calum and Duror?
5 What specific ideas does Jenkins consider in his exploration of the theme of war?
6 How is Roderick's character used to convey ideas about social class?

3.4 Language features and analysis

Target your thinking

- What does the term 'language features' mean?
- How does Jenkins use word choice and imagery to create mood or atmosphere?
- How are language features used to create a more vivid impression of the novel's settings and characters?

When demonstrating your knowledge and understanding of the novel – particularly in the Scottish text section of the exam – you will be expected to **analyse** and **evaluate** how the writer uses language to establish various aspects of the novel. For example, you may be writing about how language is used to convey aspects of setting or characters; to create atmosphere or mood; or to establish narrative points of view. If you are answering on *The Cone-Gatherers* for the Scottish text section of the exam paper, it is likely that you will be referring to techniques that require you to look at the finer details of language such as the writer's use of word choice or imagery. However, if you choose to write your critical essay on *The Cone-Gatherers*, you are likely to be taking a more holistic view of the novel and will consider broader aspects such as characterisation, setting, symbolism, plot and structure.

> ### Glossary
>
> **analyse:** to break something down into its constituent parts in order to understand how it is made or how it works. Analysis in literature means to examine a text in detail and gain an understanding of *how* the writer has used different literary techniques to create an effective piece of work.
>
> **evaluate:** to assess the effectiveness of something. Evaluation in literature means to consider how effectively the writer has achieved what he or she set out to achieve.

This means that when you are discussing *The Cone-Gatherers* as a piece of literature, it is important to show that you are aware of it as a crafted piece of work – a literary text created by a writer who has taken care in using words, sentence types and language techniques in the creation of a memorable story. Discussing a novel is about far more than simply saying *what* happens in it – you need to be able to critically appreciate the novel by saying *how* the writer has created the various aspects that make it memorable.

Language features in *The Cone-Gatherers*

You may be wondering exactly what is meant by 'language features'. You are likely to be confronted with this term when you are studying the novel and when you are responding to exam questions, so you will need to know what these features are before you can identify and comment on them. The list below gives some of the more common features of language Jenkins uses to create effects in the novel. These are features that you are likely to be discussing in your analysis and evaluation of *The Cone-Gatherers*:

- word choice
- imagery
- symbolism
- pathetic fallacy
- point of view
- dialogue

Further information on these and other language features is contained in the Glossary of literary terms at the back of this guide.

Word choice

Words are the most versatile tool in a writer's toolkit. They are one of the basic building blocks of language. By choosing words with specific **connotations**, a writer can influence how we perceive important textual elements such as characters, setting, atmosphere and tone. In *The Cone-Gatherers*, Jenkins uses description not only to tell the story but also to help us 'see' the people, places and events he describes: word choice is an effective component in these descriptions.

The information in Section 4.1 of this guide offers more developed guidance on how to deal with this language feature in the exam, but it is worthwhile examining some specific instances of where Jenkins uses word choice to create specific effects in the novel.

> **Glossary**
> **connotations:** the ideas suggested by a word; this is slightly different from the literal meaning (or denotation) of the word.

Examples of significant word choice

Look at the words used in the description of Erchie Graham's hurried journey to ask for the brothers' help:

> He had now to traverse a great Sargasso of withered leaves. Every step was a slither, and took him over the boots; one step was particularly unlucky, it landed him waist-deep in an ice-cold concealed pool. A few yards off stood a dead Chili pine, with the ground beneath littered with its fragments, like ordure.

It is clear that Jenkins wishes to show how difficult this journey is for the elderly Graham and how tricky the landscape is to navigate. For this description, therefore, he has chosen certain words to show the awkwardness of the journey. These words and their connotations are given below:

- *Sargasso* – a sea in the Atlantic Ocean that has no land boundaries and is filled with masses of floating seaweed. It is the spawning ground of several eel species. It is difficult to navigate the Sargasso Sea, and seaweed and eels are both slippery: this choice of word (imagery is also being used here) suggests the ground is tangled and slippery to move across
- *withered leaves* – suggests decay and dampness, rotten ground that makes it hard to move
- *slither* – implies danger caused by sliding and slipping movement
- *unlucky* – gives a sense of an ill-fated journey
- *ice-cold* – suggests something inhospitable and dangerous
- *concealed* – hints at something menacing and lurking under the surface
- *dead* – suggests a threatening barren landscape
- *fragments* – suggests breakage and fragility, decay
- *ordure* – means dung or refuse, and this suggests the rottenness of the tree as well as the landscape

It is easy to see that the connotations of these words make Graham's journey seem like a particularly difficult one. If Jenkins had not chosen these words with great care, we would not have had such a clear impression of Graham's struggle to reach the brothers and the setting in this part of the woods.

Word choice is also a language feature that can be used to create 'atmosphere' or mood. When the imaginative Roderick goes to the woods with the cake for Calum and Neil, he is caught up with the woods' atmosphere of mystery yet is slightly afraid of the menace he finds in the dim solitude. Jenkins creates a mood of mystery and menace by choosing certain words for the description of the woods. These words with strong connotations are highlighted in the following extract:

> Therefore there was magic and terror. The wood was enchanted, full of terrifying presences. A knot in a tree glowered like a green face. Low-hanging branches were evil birds swooping with talons ready to rip his face and pluck out his eyes…Here were clusters of juniper, grey with fungus, jungles of withered willow herb, taller than himself, piles of dead leaves like graves…

Build critical skills

Try substituting some less descriptive words into the description of Graham's journey, such as 'stretch' instead of 'Sargasso' and 'hard' instead of 'a slither'. This should allow you to see how Jenkins' apt choice of words makes the journey seem much more vivid.

Build critical skills

Jenkins also uses word choice to give us a clear impression of characters. Choose descriptions of one or two characters and note how the writer's use of word choice conveys key aspects of these characters.

Imagery

In literature, **imagery** – sometimes referred to as figurative language – is a technique in which an author uses comparisons to represent people, places, objects or ideas. Often, these comparisons appeal to some aspect of our senses and this gives us a clearer mental 'image' or 'picture' of the thing being described. **Similes** and **metaphors** are perhaps the most common form of imagery used in *The Cone-Gatherers*. For example, Jenkins often uses similes and metaphors that rely on animals to convey aspects of Calum's character. Calum is described as being 'as indigenous as a squirrel or bird', 'a deer hunted by remorseless men' and is 'as agile as any monkey'. Jenkins uses this imagery to convey Calum's affinity with the natural world and to give us a clearer picture of his ease when in the trees.

> **Glossary**
>
> **imagery:** a technique, sometimes referred to as 'figurative language', used to stimulate understanding of things, ideas or people through comparisons with, for example, objects, often in original and surprising ways. Popular examples are simile and metaphor.
>
> **simile:** a comparison where one thing is said to be like another thing with similar qualities. Similes often use 'like…' or 'as…as…' to make the comparison.
>
> **metaphor:** a comparison in which a writer says (or implies) one thing *is* another thing, both sides of the comparison sharing a similar quality.

Imagery is used throughout the novel to create different effects. Like word choice, imagery can be used to evoke settings, convey aspects of character, create atmosphere and enhance our understanding of the novel's themes. Imagery and symbolism are closely linked, with imagery often being used to carry symbolic significance. For example, imagery can be used to describe a character who then becomes a symbol of something far more abstract. One example of this in *The Cone-Gatherers* is the repeated image of a dying tree which is often used to describe Duror, who becomes the symbolic representation of evil in the novel.

Key quotation

Duror: 'He was like a tree still straight, still showing green leaves; but underground death was creeping along the roots.'

Symbolism

Symbolism means the use of symbols – in literature, this often involves imagery – to represent ideas or qualities. In *The Cone-Gatherers*, we have already seen that characters can act as symbols for ideas: Calum symbolises goodness; Duror symbolises evil; Lady Runcie-Campbell could be said to symbolise the upper classes and the established social order. However, it is not only characters who act as symbols: there are other instances where symbolism is used to highlight important ideas and to convey key themes. Significant symbols in *The Cone-Gatherers* include:

- the cones
- the silver firs
- the doll

The cones

The cones that Calum and Neil are sent to gather represent new hope and regeneration, two of the central ideas within the novel. They also symbolise nature. Cones are mentioned in the first and final paragraphs, emphasising the cycles of nature as well as adding to the novel's structural cohesion.

On the first page of the novel, the cones Calum collects are described as 'sweet' and 'resinous', and at other places they are described as 'golden', suggesting that they have positive qualities and are valuable. This idea of the cones' great worth and their ability to bring better things is seen in the later image of Calum and Neil 'plucking nuts of sunshine' (the cones) while the sun shines down upon the trees where the brothers work. Calum is the brother most connected with the cones. During the storm and in the beach hut, Calum refuses to leave his bag of cones while Neil leaves his bag behind in the tree. This emphasises Calum's close bond with nature and, just like the cones, his potential to bring hope for the future. Even after Calum's murder, the cones remain a symbol of promise: as they fall to earth with the drops of Calum's blood, there is a suggestion that they are being planted and watered, the falling cones symbolising the new hope that comes to the estate after Duror's evil has been removed by Calum's sacrifice.

The silver firs

We are told that the silver firs are among 'the tallest' on the estate and they form a barrier that screens the Runcie-Campbells' house from the world outside. As such, they symbolise the social barriers that separate the upper classes from the middle and working classes who serve them. When Tulloch asks Lady Runcie-Campbell for permission to gather the silver fir cones, she does not immediately grant it, telling him that she will consider his request. Her reason for this seems to be that she wishes to keep the lowly cone-gatherers at a distance and fears that they will be too near to the house if allowed into the silver firs. Thus, the physical barrier of the silver firs symbolises the social barriers placed between the classes.

The tops of the silver firs seem 'inaccessible', yet Roderick manages to reach the uppermost reaches. In the light of Roderick's fairness and attitude towards those of a lower class than himself, his ascent of the silver firs could be viewed as a symbol of him having the potential to breach the barrier between the classes. It is Manson, a humble ploughboy, who helps Roderick down from the silver fir tree, suggesting perhaps that class barriers – as represented by the silver firs – can be broken only when those of different classes work together to achieve a common goal.

The doll

In Calum and Tulloch's hands, the broken doll from the beach hut – which had originally belonged to Sheila – is a symbol of innocence. Calum holds the doll 'tenderly', showing his respect for it and his intention to repair it. When Tulloch takes the doll from a distressed Lady Runcie-Campbell after Duror has been making obscene allegations, he says his young daughter will be 'delighted with it'. In Duror's hands, the doll is described as 'an obscene symbol', yet in Tulloch's hands it becomes 'innocent again' – a simple toy to please a young child.

Calum's simple and childlike view of the world means that he is an innocent, with no awareness of the darkness of the adult world. The same could be said of Tulloch's young daughter – a child who has no awareness of life's evils. Duror, however, is corrupted by frustrated desires and evil thoughts. Connected with the character who holds it, the doll – discarded by Sheila, who is now growing up and caught between childhood innocence and knowledge of the adult world – is a symbol of both the innocence of childhood and the darkness of the adult world.

Pathetic fallacy

▲ The indigo clouds of the approaching storm signal the turbulence to come for Calum and Neil

Strictly speaking, **pathetic fallacy** is a specific kind of **personification**. This language feature is one in which the natural world seems to reflect the emotions or events occurring within the text – often the weather acts as a suitable backdrop for characters' feelings or key incidents.

Examples of pathetic fallacy

Jenkins makes effective use of pathetic fallacy in several places. Chapter 5 begins with a description of bright sunshine that reflects the brothers' happiness before Duror's arrival; in Chapter 11, the dramatic description of the storm's arrival heralds the dreadful events in the beach hut. When the storm arrives, the atmosphere of excitement is instantly replaced by one of bleakness and fear. As Neil and Calum watch from their place in the trees, they see that 'Black clouds were now overhead…Colour faded from the wood…' and this echoes their dark thoughts and fears, in addition to setting a bleak tone suited to their eviction from the beach hut. The use of pathetic fallacy here shows the thunder personified as a wild beast, the wind as a violent individual intent on damaging the trees, and the trees themselves as being sullen and depressed: Jenkins describes how 'Thunder snarled…A sough of wind shook the gloomy host of trees'. The description of the incoming storm reflects Calum and Neil's terror at their vulnerable position high in the treetops, as well as suggesting the turbulence of the events to come in the beach hut.

Of course, pathetic fallacy can also be used to reflect positive emotions and to create a happy mood. When the brothers are gathering cones before Duror arrives to tell them about the deer drive, the sun is shining brightly on the loch and the cones and water are glittering with promise. This upbeat description of the weather finds a parallel in Neil and Calum's mood: Neil is singing and Calum is lost in 'so much present joy'. When Duror approaches the brothers, however, he walks through 'sunshine and shadow', suggesting his potential to bring darkness.

Point of view

Although **point of view**, or narrative stance as it is sometimes called, is often thought of as a structural technique, it is also worth considering this aspect of the novel when analysing and evaluating the writer's use of language. Point of view has already been mentioned briefly in the Plot and structure section of this guide, with the narrative stance identified as that of an omniscient third-person narrator.

Use of an omniscient third-person narrator

A third-person narrator is removed from the action of the novel and is therefore able to tell the story from an outsider's point of view. Since the narrator is not a character in the story, this type of narration allows for an unbiased view of events. Third-person narration can sometimes be a simple blow-by-blow account of events, with no insight into each character's emotions; this is known as limited third-person narration. However, Jenkins uses an omniscient third-person 'voice' to tell the story, giving us the widest view of what is happening as we are able to see each character's thoughts and feelings. In *The Cone-Gatherers*, this is a particularly important narrative choice as Duror's mental state is not immediately obvious from his initially calm exterior. The frequent insights we are given into his thoughts convince us of his escalating frustrations and deteriorating mental health.

Duror's horror towards physical imperfections is one of the main reasons for his hatred of Calum, but we would never be aware of this aspect of his personality if the narrative point of view did not allow us to see that 'since childhood [Duror] had been repelled by anything living that had an imperfection'. The narrator also allows us to see Duror's secret approval of the Nazis' use of gas chambers, alerting us to the terrible darkness and cruelty that lie within his character.

We learn a great deal about Duror from Jenkins' use of this narrative stance, but this point of view also gives us a greater appreciation of Lady Runcie-Campbell's background and the social class she inhabits. When thinking of Roderick's compassion, we see her thoughts on both her father, the judge, and her husband, the aristocrat. This allows us to make up our own minds about how far she has been influenced by their conflicting views. She sees her father as a 'corrupter' of Roderick's upper-class inheritance and reminds Roderick that his father has repeatedly told him of 'the supreme importance of asserting [his] inherited position'. This suggests that the values of the upper-class world are a very strong influence on her, yet we also see her doubts when, rushing to ask for the brothers' help, she realises that 'Whatever she ought to feel, anger seemed wrong and unavailing'. In the narrator's revelation of her thoughts, we can see that Lady Runcie-Campbell recognises her own part in the tragedy.

Dialogue

Although **dialogue** is often associated with drama, it is also an essential component in almost all novels. A writer's use of dialogue can provide insight into the nature of a novel's characters and settings. This is certainly true in *The Cone-Gatherers*, where dialogue is used to convey aspects of character as well as highlighting some of the central concerns. We gain valuable information about characters from what they say to others – and sometimes from what they do not say. Calum is a major character in the novel, but his dialogue with other characters is limited. This helps us to view him as a simple man who is happy to let Neil take

> **Glossary**
> **dialogue:** conversation between characters.

Key quotation

'I tell you,' went on Neil, with passion, crushing a cone in his fist, 'she cannot one day treat us as lower than dogs, and next day order us to do her bidding. We will starve first. If she wishes our help, let her come and ask for it.'

Glossary

colloquialisms: informal words or phrases; slang words.

care of the day-to-day responsibilities. Calum is also more at home in the natural world, surrounded by trees and animals, than in the human world – so his short sentences and shy comments reflect his innocent and childlike character. On the other hand, Neil has more to say for himself. Neil's frustrations and his preoccupation with survival in a world that seems unfair to the less fortunate are seen in his dialogue at various points in the novel. He talks to Calum about the inequalities of the world. In the hotel bar he is seen 'talking importantly to a man from Ardmore' and his speech to Erchie Graham reveals his passionate belief in equal rights.

Erchie Graham often uses **colloquialisms** in his speech, illustrating his working-class status. He asks Neil if he is 'daft', occasionally uses blasphemies and adopts an informal tone when moaning to the other beaters in the deer hunt. This makes it clear that he is not well educated and is from a lower-class background. Mrs Lochie uses Scots words such as 'aye', 'ken' and 'ain' in her dialogue with Duror and Lady Runcie-Campbell. The use of these words associates her with the local area, as well as indicating her working-class background: the upper class in Scotland at that time would have been aware of the Scots language but would not have used it in conversation.

In contrast, Lady Runcie-Campbell's speech reveals her established position as a member of the upper-class community. In dialogue with other characters, she often issues commands, showing that she is in a position of authority and is comfortable with her elevated social status. Her vocabulary is much greater than that of all the other characters in the story, again emphasising her educated and wealthy background. In almost all of her conversations with others, she is the first person to speak, suggesting that she is the person most in control of things. The only times when she does not speak first are during her final meeting with Duror and in her brief conversation with Mrs Morton when told of Roderick's predicament in the tree. Mrs Morton does knock on the door before entering, however, showing Lady Runcie-Campbell's position of power. In her final dialogue with Duror, the reversal of the normal order of their conversation – despite Duror's first words being an untruthful apology – highlights her inability to control her gamekeeper.

Duror's participation in dialogue is often minimal, suggesting his gradual withdrawal from society into the darkness of his own mind. His contributions to conversations are often terse, and his replies to Mrs Lochie and the doctor's questions exemplify his dour personality and his determination to bottle up the frustrations of his life. In several conversations, his speech is described as 'mumbling' and he is 'incoherent'. His confused comments after his nightmare of Peggy being pecked to death by the thrushes, his rambling speech after the savage killing of the deer and the 'repetitious incoherence' in his final conversation with Lady Runcie-Campbell and Tulloch all indicate his growing instability and foreshadow the tragic events at the novel's end.

REVIEW YOUR LEARNING

(Answers are given on p. 109.)

1 Name three language features that Jenkins uses in *The Cone-Gatherers*.
2 Explain what 'connotation' means.
3 What is a metaphor?
4 Explain what is meant by the term 'imagery'.
5 Give an example of a symbol from the text and explain how it is used in the novel.
6 What is 'pathetic fallacy'?
7 What narrative stance does Jenkins use in *The Cone-Gatherers*?
8 How does Jenkins use dialogue to add to our understanding of the novel?

4 Approaching the Critical Reading paper

The Critical Reading paper

For both National 5 and Higher levels, the time allocated for this part of the exam is 1 hour and 30 minutes. The Critical Reading paper is divided into two sections – you should spend approximately 45 minutes on each. Each section is worth 20 marks, giving an overall total of 40 marks for this paper.

- Section 1: Scottish text – in this section, you will read an extract taken from one of the set Scottish texts and then answer some shorter questions on that extract and one longer question on the text overall.

- Section 2: Critical essay – in this section, you will write one critical essay on a text that you have previously studied from the genres of drama, prose, poetry, film and television drama or language.

> ### Exam tip
> The Scottish text is sometimes called different things such as the Scottish set text or Scottish textual analysis.

Selecting your texts

It is important to remember that both National 5 and Higher levels have rules that may affect your choice of section when writing on *The Cone-Gatherers*. You will be able to see these rules if you look at the front page of any National 5 or Higher past paper. If you have studied two or more of the texts specified on SQA's list of Scottish texts, you will have to think carefully when choosing your preferred text for each section.

The rules of the paper state that:

- you cannot answer on the same text in Sections 1 and 2
- you must answer on a different genre in each section

4.1 Critical Reading Section 1: Scottish text

Target your thinking

- How many marks are allocated for the Scottish text section?
- What should you consider when 'decoding' the Scottish text questions?
- How can planning lead to more effective answers for the Scottish text questions?
- What does 'commonality' mean?
- How should you set out your answer for the Scottish text final question?
- What do you have to do to achieve the best marks?

Introduction to the Scottish text

- Make sure you know the novel really well. You should have an accurate knowledge of 'the Five Ws' (**W**here and **W**hen is the novel set? **W**hat happens? **W**ho is involved? **W**hy do these events happen?).
- Make sure you have a clear understanding of the novel's theme(s).
- Remember that a great deal of what you have learned when studying for the RUAE paper is transferable to this paper and will also have given you the skills to recognise and comment on language features. These skills are likely to be useful when answering the shorter questions.
- Read the extract carefully before you look at the questions.
- You may find it helpful to highlight anything you think is significant in the extract such as powerful word choice, imagery, important sections of dialogue or vivid descriptions. Highlighting in this way is likely to be useful when you are deciding how to set out your answers.

> If you are studying at National 5, read the information below. If you are studying at Higher level, turn to page 77.

Advice for National 5

This section of the exam paper tests your knowledge and understanding of the Scottish text you have studied. A total of 20 marks is available for this section. This is 50% of the Critical Reading paper and 20% of your overall mark. You will be asked:

- several short questions on an extract from the novel, worth a total of 12 marks
- a final, more extended question that requires you to show your knowledge of the whole text, worth 8 marks

At National 5 level, the extract will be roughly 30 lines of text. The questions will usually ask you to 'explain' something seen in the lines you are asked to look at, for example a character's feelings; an atmosphere that is created; a relationship; a setting. You may also be asked to 'identify' something in these lines. The extract you are given will provide plenty of opportunities to choose examples that you can then use in your 'explanation'.

The extract will also deal with the topic you are asked to look at in the 8-mark question. This question will usually ask you to 'show how' the writer presents a 'bigger' aspect of the text, for example a character, a theme, an idea or the use of a specific feature such as imagery.

Sample extract and questions

The following extract is typical of what you will find in the exam. Read it carefully before looking at the advice on questions that follow.

On Saturday the beneficent weather continued: frost at dawn, iridescence and gold at noon, and afterwards blue skies, warmth, and astonished singing of birds. That morning, however, Neil chose to work in a Douglas fir tree; the darkness amidst its evergreen branches suited
5 his mood.

Since the deer drive he had been bitter and rebellious. When Mr Tulloch, with much satisfaction at his own diplomacy and admiration of the lady's sense of fairness, had told them they were to be allowed to stay on in the wood provided they kept out of everybody's way, Neil
10 had listened with eyes on the ground and lips tight: not for Calum's sake even could he at that moment have admitted they owed the lady gratitude. Afterwards, in walking to the hut, he had burst out into a passionate denunciation of the lady and what she stood for. Seizing Calum fiercely, he had dragged him out of the way of a bush whose
15 outermost twigs he might have brushed against in passing, and had shouted that surely he had heard what Mr Tulloch had said, they were to keep out of the way, they were to provoke nobody, they were to be like insects, not bees or ants which could sting and bite, but tiny flies which could do no harm since there was nothing in creation so
20 feeble as not to be able to molest them. Calum, already bewildered and miserable, had not understood; into his sobs had come entreaty, but this time Neil had not yielded.

Nor had he yielded by Saturday. When Calum accidentally tore off a spray of the Douglas fir and was smelling its fragrance, Neil caught
25 sight of him.

'Is that a cone?'

Calum, puzzled, looked at the green spray in his hand.

'I asked you, is that a cone?'

Calum shook his head. He smiled. 'No Neil, it's just a bit of branch. It
30 came off. I couldn't help it.'

'You're here to collect cones, that's all,' yelled Neil. 'You're to do nothing
else. How often have I to tell you that? Didn't you hear Mr Tulloch
himself say it?'

'But I couldn't help it, Neil.'

35 'The likes of you and me have just got to help it, when our betters tell
us. You can't even have an accident and fall from this tree. Do you
ken why? Because the lady would get to hear about it, and she'd be
annoyed; she'd be annoyed because you'd broken your neck and spilled
your blood on her land.'

Now you have read the extract carefully, look at the following questions.
These are similar to the types of questions you will see in the exam. In
the next part we will consider how to tackle these questions.

1 Look at lines 1–5.

   By referring to **one** example, explain how the writer suggests
   good aspects of the weather. (2 marks)

2 Look at lines 6–22.

   By referring to **two** examples, explain how the writer makes it
   clear that Neil is angry. (4 marks)

3 Look at lines 23–34.

   By referring to **two** examples, explain how Neil and Calum's
   different personalities are made clear. (4 marks)

4 Look at lines 35–39.

   By referring to **one** example, identify one reason for Neil's
   frustration. (2 marks)

5 By referring to this extract and to elsewhere in the novel, show
   how the theme of social class is explored. (8 marks)

Answering the shorter questions

'Decoding' the questions

The first thing to be aware of is that the shorter questions are set out
in a way that will actually help you answer correctly. You may not have
realised it, but it is possible to 'decode' the questions. This will help you to
give an answer that is relevant and of an appropriate length.

Using the correct lines

Each of the shorter questions has a similar structure: there is a first sentence containing the instruction to 'Look at lines…', which is then followed by a second sentence containing the actual question. It is important that you look at the lines indicated in that first instruction and that you *only* select your answer choices from these lines. You will not gain any marks for answers taken from outside the lines stated in the question.

Checking the mark allocation

The second thing you should look at is the number of marks stated at the end of the question. This is a good indication of how much detail, or how many quotations/references and comments, you should include in your answer.

The 12 marks available for the shorter Scottish text questions will be made up of a combination of questions worth 2 marks and 4 marks. These questions are marked on the basis that an appropriate quotation/ reference = 1 mark and then an appropriate comment on that reference = 1 mark. In questions worth 4 marks, you will see the phrase 'By referring to **two** examples…' – the bold text is used to highlight the number of references with comment that you need to make.

Identifying the focus of the question

The last thing you should be aware of in each question is the 'focus', i.e. exactly *what* you are being asked to look for. At National 5, the questions will usually ask you to 'explain' or 'identify' a particular focus. Make sure you pay careful attention to whatever aspect of the text you are being asked to 'explain' or 'identify'. For example, Question 1 above is an analysis question that focuses on 'good aspects of the weather'.

When you have read the extract carefully and looked over all of the accompanying questions, you will be well placed to start answering this part of the exam paper. There is no 'right' or 'wrong' way of setting out your answers: some candidates opt to answer the shorter questions using linked sentences; others opt for a bullet-point approach. It is, however, important to make sure that your answers are structured in a way that makes your thoughts clear to the marker.

Now let's take a detailed look at the following questions with their accompanying answers and commentaries. These will demonstrate how you should tackle this type of shorter question at National 5 level.

Tackling some sample questions

> 1 Look at lines 1–4.
>
> By referring to **one** example, explain how the writer suggests good aspects of the weather. (2 marks)

There are 2 marks available:

- 1 mark for selecting an appropriate reference suggesting 'good aspects of the weather'
- 1 mark for commenting on/explaining how the reference 'suggests good aspects of the weather'

Keep the focus of the question firmly in mind. You are looking to select and comment on a part of the text that 'suggests good aspects of the weather'.

There are plenty of possibilities for answers here. The most obvious are:

- 'frost at dawn' suggests a crisp and clean start to the day
- 'iridescence' suggests a beautiful light and attractive changing colours
- 'gold' has connotations of something valuable and precious
- 'blue skies' suggests warmth and summer, a lack of obstacles
- 'warmth' has connotations of being welcoming and comforting
- 'singing of birds' has connotations of spring and summer, seasons of promise, and of happiness and melody

Sample answer

The writer suggests good aspects of the weather by describing the 'gold' (1) of noon time, suggesting something beautiful and precious and showing that the weather is pleasant and something enjoyed by Neil and Calum (1).

This answer would gain full marks. The candidate then makes a comment on the positive connotations of gold. This is an appropriate reference that would gain 1 mark. The candidate makes a relevant comment on the connotations of gold to suggest something positive.

> 3 Look at lines 18–27.
>
> By referring to **two** examples, explain how Neil and Calum's different personalities are made clear. (4 marks)

Remember the number of marks available – 4 marks means that you need to select two references that suggest 'how Neil and Calum's different personalities are made clear' and then make appropriate comments on how each of your chosen references suggests their personalities.

Keep the focus of the question firmly in mind. You are looking to select and comment on parts of the text that suggest 'Neil and Calum's different personalities'. As this question is worth 4 marks and it asks about 'different personalities', for full marks it is essential that you deal with how both characters are depicted in order to show the difference, i.e. make a comment on how Neil's personality is portrayed and then make a separate comment on how Calum's personality is portrayed.

You could consider the following possibilities:

Neil:

- 'Is that a cone?'/'I asked you, is that a cone?'/'How often have I to tell you that?' – the repeated use of questions suggests Neil is in charge and is interrogating Calum
- 'I asked you...' suggests Neil is in control of the situation/is assertive or determined
- 'yelled' has connotations of being in charge and bossing someone around, suggesting Neil is dominant

Calum:

- 'puzzled' suggests confusion and bewilderment, showing Calum does not fully understand what is happening around him
- 'looked at the green spray in his hand' – Calum needs to check what he is holding when Neil questions him, showing his lack of confidence in himself
- 'smiled' has connotations of being good-natured or happy

Sample answer

Neil and Calum's different personalities are shown by:

Neil's repeated questions to Calum: 'Is that a cone?' and 'I asked you, is that a cone?' (1) seem almost aggressive (1) and suggest that he dominates his brother and is quite a determined character.

Calum: 'puzzled' (1) suggests he is easily confused when Neil asks a simple question about the cone, showing he is not as quick as Neil (1).

This answer would gain full marks. The candidate has selected two appropriate references – one for each personality – and makes sensible comments on how each reference shows the difference in Neil and Calum's personalities. The candidate chooses to deal with word choice and sentence structure – perfectly acceptable choices for a question that asks candidates to 'explain how'.

> ### Exam tip
> Now that you have seen some examples of the level of response required to answer the shorter Scottish text questions successfully, you can practise your skills by attempting Questions 2 and 4 on this extract.

Answering the 8-mark question

The 8-mark question allows you to show that you can link the extract with your wider knowledge of the entire novel.

First, it is important that you are aware of how the question is marked. The marks for this question are allocated as follows:

- 2 marks are given for identifying elements of '**commonality**'
- 2 marks are given for linking the question **to the extract** – 1 mark for the quotation/reference + 1 mark for the comment
- 4 marks are given for linking the question **to elsewhere in the novel** – 1 mark for the quotation/reference + 1 mark for the comment (× 2)

Tackling the sample question

Let's take a closer look at the 8-mark question for the above extract:

> 5 By referring to this extract and to elsewhere in the novel, show how the theme of social class is explored. (8 marks)

Identifying elements of 'commonality'

'Commonality' is provided for you in the question's focus. The 8-mark question will ask you to consider some aspect of the text such as a theme, a character or the use of a literary feature or technique. This aspect of the text – the focus of the question – is 'commonality' and what you have to do in this first part of the question is identify elements of this 'commonality' within *The Cone-Gatherers*. This means that you should take a broad view of the text and identify some parts of the novel where you have seen this focus. What you will write in your answer depends on the question's focus. You may have to look for a particular piece of characterisation, an incident, a setting or the use of a technique, but the two things you identify in this part of your answer must have 'commonality' in terms of the question.

It is clear that the focus or 'commonality' of this question is 'the theme of social class'. You should aim to answer this part of the question by identifying two places where Jenkins deals with the theme of social class. A good approach is to identify where the focus can be seen in the extract given in the exam paper and then to identify another place in the book where this focus can be found in the wider text.

Sample paragraph

The theme of social class is seen when the upper-class Lady Runcie-Campbell has the power to 'allow' the cone-gatherers to remain in the woods. Lower-class characters like Neil or Calum have almost no power to stand up to her.

In this part on 'commonality', the candidate has taken the successful approach of looking at the extract first and then identifying Lady Runcie-Campbell as a powerful member of the upper class who can 'allow' Neil and Calum to stay in the woods. The candidate then takes a wider view of the text and identifies Neil and Calum as members of the lower class with far less power than Lady Runcie-Campbell. Both of these points are acceptable comments for 'commonality' and would gain 1 mark each.

Linking the question to the extract

The 2 marks given for this part of the question are awarded for discussing how the focus is shown within the extract. You should answer this part of the question by quoting/referring to where 'social class' is shown in the extract and then commenting on how your selected reference links to the theme of social class.

Sample paragraph

In the extract, we learn that Neil was angry at 'the lady and what she stood for' even when the brothers were allowed to stay in the woods (1). He is angry because she is powerful and can control every bit of their lives — from where they live to what they do in the woods (1).

The candidate has selected a quotation/reference that links to the idea of the different social classes and then makes an appropriate comment on why Neil is angry at this difference. This is an acceptable answer for the 'linking the question to the extract' part of the question.

Linking the question to elsewhere in the novel

Although this part of the question requires you to take a similar approach to the one taken for the extract, it is important to remember that this section is worth 4 marks. This means that two appropriate quotations/references from elsewhere in the novel are needed, along with an appropriate comment for each reference. You are being asked to dip into your overall knowledge of *The Cone-Gatherers* in order to select appropriate quotations/references and comment on how these references relate to the focus of the question. This may seem a daunting task, but you are not expected to be able to quote directly from such a large text: you may remember a useful quotation that links well with the focus of the question, but it is also fine if you use your own words when explaining a relevant aspect of the text.

Sample paragraph

Elsewhere in the novel, we see the theme of social class shown when Lady Runcie-Campbell worries that Roderick is too friendly with the cone-gatherers and the servants who are of a lower class

*than the Runcie-Campbell family (1). She worries about Roderick
because this is not acceptable behaviour for a baronet's son (1).*

*Roderick tells his mother that he thinks they should offer the cone-
gatherers 'a lift' (1), showing that he does not seem to believe in
class barriers (1).*

The candidate has selected two relevant references (one of which has an
accompanying quotation) dealing with the different attitudes to class:
one reference to Lady Runcie-Campbell's worries about Roderick and
the other reference to Roderick's actions. Both of these references are
appropriate, as are the accompanying explanations/comments, so this
answer would achieve (1 + 1) for the first reference and comment and
then (1 + 1) for the second reference and comment. This is a successful
answer that fulfils all the requirements of this part of the question.

Setting out your answer

There is no 'right' or 'wrong' way of setting out your answer. You can
write a mini-essay or use bullet points for this question. However, it may
help you to clarify exactly what you wish to say in each section if you
structure your answer using headings that reflect how it will be marked
(such as Commonality, Extract and Elsewhere), or start each section of
your answer by referring to these sections.

Advice for Higher

This section of the paper tests your knowledge and understanding of the
specified Scottish text you have studied, as well as your analytical and
evaluative skills. A total of 20 marks is available for this section. This is
50% of the Critical Reading paper and 20% of your overall mark. You will
be asked:

- three short questions on an extract from the novel, worth a total of
  10 marks
- a final, more extended question that requires you to demonstrate your
  knowledge of the entire text, worth 10 marks

At Higher level, the extract will usually be about 50 lines of text. It will
provide plenty of opportunity to answer shorter questions on the writer's
use of language, as well as providing a focus on a wider aspect of the text
such as an element of characterisation, a theme or the use of a specific
literary feature.

> **Exam tip**
>
> It is important to remember that at Higher level, unlike National 5, you
> are not awarded any marks for simply selecting an appropriate quotation
> or textual reference: you must make a relevant comment on how your
> chosen reference meets the specific point noted in the question.

Sample extract and questions

The following extract is typical of what you will find in the exam. Read it carefully before looking at the advice on the questions that follow.

The doctor's house was the second last villa beyond the pier. At that point, just where the road was about to end in the wilderness of the shore, the first glimpse of the open sea was got, with the far-off twinkle of the lighthouse.

5   There Duror paused. Whin bushes, profusely golden in summer, stirred rustily in the breeze. Against the darkling sky he saw in the doctor's garden one of the palm trees grown in this mild northern land; and further off, with even stronger temptation of distance, were stars, so remote, and so oblivious of his infinitely petty existence that for a few
10 moments he experienced rest and hope. Sweat broke out over his body. Gazing towards the doctor's lighted window he thought that perhaps the old man might be able to prescribe some powder or pills to induce not sleep only but an awakening into a life where he could again touch the elm tree before he entered his house.

15 As the hope faded, and the lighthouse's beam strengthened, he recalled his travail under that elm after the deer drive. The shooting-brake had set him and his dogs down outside his house. The sun had been shining and birds singing. Only a few paces across the white shingle was his gate. There were still some flowers on the fuchsia bushes. Suddenly
20 over the whole scene had dropped darkness, in the midst of which the birds had continued to sing, but without purpose, desolately. He could not move; he was as powerless as the elm beside him; and for those two or three minutes he had felt his sap, poisoned, flowing out of him into the dark earth. His dogs had whined up at him in bewilderment, alarm,
25 and love; they had growled at the enemy persecuting him, which they could sense but not see.

By the whins then, empty of hope, he knew there was one thing on earth he did not want ever again to see; the smile of the hunchback. He swung from it as a pony from an adder. So vivid was his horror of
30 seeing it that he actually shut his eyes there on the darkening road; but there were eyes within him he could not close at will, and these now began to see that smile, and only that smile.

It was the doctor's wife who admitted him. She was a small white-haired woman in black. The sadness of her face was a joke amongst
35 those patients whose ailments were trifling; others, fearful that their pains might be diagnosed as mortal, saw no cause for smiles in her prophetic dejection.

'The doctor's waiting for you in the surgery, Mr Duror,' she said.

Crossing to the surgery door, she knocked on it and waited till her
40 husband opened it.

He was, on the contrary, as effervescent as if, a minute ago he had just
discovered a panacea. Duror smelled whisky.

'I've brought you some venison, doctor,' he said, 'with Lady Runcie-
Campbell's compliments.'

45 The doctor snatched it and began to dandle it, as if it was new-born
baby and he its delighted father.

This, thought Duror, is the man on whom I have to depend for a cure.

Now you have read the extract carefully, look at the following questions.
These are similar to the types of questions you will see in the exam. In
the next part we will consider how to tackle these questions.

1 Look at lines 1–14.

   By referring to **at least two** examples, analyse how the writer's
   use of language creates a lonely mood. (4 marks)

2 Look at lines 15–32.

   By referring to **at least two** examples, analyse how the writer's
   use of language conveys Duror's despair. (4 marks)

3 Look at lines 33–47.

   Analyse how the writer's use of language conveys the difference
   between the doctor and his wife. (2 marks)

4 By referring to this extract and to elsewhere in the novel, discuss
   how Jenkins explores the theme of isolation. (10 marks)

Answering the shorter questions

'Decoding' the questions

The first thing to be aware of is that the shorter questions are set out
in a way that will actually help you answer correctly. You may not
have realised it, but it is possible to 'decode' the questions so that you
have some help in providing an answer which is relevant and is of an
appropriate length.

Using the correct lines

Each of the shorter questions has a similar structure: there is a first
sentence containing the instruction to 'Look at lines…', which is then
followed by a second sentence containing the actual question. It is
important that you look over the lines indicated in that first instruction

and that you *only* select your answer choices from these lines. You will not gain any marks for answers taken from outside the lines stated in the question.

Checking the mark allocation

The second thing you should look at is the number of marks stated at the end of the question. This is a good indication of how much detail, or how many quotations/references and comments, you should include in your answer.

Usually, the 10 marks available for the shorter Scottish text questions will be made up of a combination of questions worth 2 marks and 4 marks, although there is a chance that you may see questions that are worth 3 marks. Note that questions worth 4 marks contain the phrase 'By referring to **at least two** examples…' – the bold text is used to highlight the *minimum* number of points you should make in your answer. Although it is possible to gain 2 marks for a detailed or insightful comment on a selected reference, it is a good idea to match the number of points you are making to the marks allocated for that question. In practice, this means that you should aim to make 2 points for a question worth 2 marks, 4 points for a question worth 4 marks, etc. Using this strategy will ensure that you have a better chance of obtaining the maximum number of marks.

Identifying the focus of the question

The last thing you should be aware of in each question is the 'focus', i.e. exactly *what* you are being asked to look for. At Higher, the questions will usually ask you to 'analyse', but occasionally you may be asked to 'explain'. 'Analyse' means exactly the same in the Critical Reading paper as it does in the RUAE paper. You need to pick out specific features of language or literary techniques and then comment on *how* these features/techniques achieve or contribute to the focus of the question. For example, Question 1 above is an analysis question that focuses on 'a lonely mood'.

When you have read the extract carefully and looked over all of the accompanying questions, you will be well placed to start answering this part of the paper. There is no 'right' or 'wrong' way of setting out your answers: some candidates opt to answer the shorter questions using linked sentences; others opt for a bullet-point approach. It is, however, important to make sure that your answers are structured in a way that makes your thoughts clear to the marker.

Now let's take a detailed look at the following questions with their accompanying answers and commentaries. These will demonstrate how you should tackle this type of 'shorter' question at Higher level.

Tackling some sample questions

> 1 Look at lines 1–11.
>
>   By referring to **at least two** examples, analyse how the writer's use of language creates a lonely mood. (4 marks)

Remember: 4 marks means that it would be wisest to make 4 points in your answer.

Keep the focus of the question firmly in mind. You are looking to select and comment on parts of the text that create 'a lonely mood'.

There are plenty of possibilities for answers here. The most obvious are:

- 'second last' suggests being close to the end, removed from the centre
- 'beyond' suggests being out of reach, far away
- 'beyond the pier' suggests the expanse of the ocean and vast journeys into the unknown
- a 'wilderness' is a place with no human habitation, wild and untamed lands that often form a natural barrier of some kind, suggesting alienation
- 'open sea' has connotations of vastness and vulnerability in a potentially hostile place
- 'far-off' has connotations of being at a great distance, removed from others
- 'rustily' suggests something decaying or which has not been in use for a long time
- 'northern land' has connotations of bleakness, cold and the far reaches of a continent
- 'stars, so remote, and so oblivious…' – obviously both 'remote' and 'oblivious' could be suitable for comment, but the repetition of 'so' also helps to emphasise the great distances Duror is contemplating

Sample answer

The writer creates a lonely mood by stating that the doctor's house was 'the second last villa', suggesting that it is almost forgotten at the end of the road and is less obvious than the other houses and therefore not really a part of the rest of the town (1).

He uses 'wilderness' to describe the shore by the house. Just as a 'wilderness' is a wild or overgrown place that does not receive any human attention, so the area around the shore is an untended, wild and isolated place that has no visitors (1).

When Duror sees the palm tree, he thinks of it as being in a 'northern land'. This has connotations of a cold and bleak place that is inhospitable and at the farthest ends of the Earth where no one lives (1).

Duror also sees the stars as 'remote', which emphasises how distant they are and suggests that he feels very far away, removed from everything and insignificant (1).

This answer would gain full marks. There are four appropriate quotations/references, along with appropriate comments on how each of these references creates 'a lonely mood'. The candidate chooses to deal with word choice and imagery – perfectly acceptable choices for a question that asks about the writer's use of language. The comments make valid and reasonably developed points on connotations associated with 'a lonely mood'.

> 3 Look at lines 26–37.
>
> Analyse how the writer's use of language conveys the difference between the doctor and his wife. (2 marks)

Remember the number of marks available – 2 marks means that it would be wisest to make 2 points in your answer. Obviously, your answer to this question is likely to be shorter than your answers to questions 1 and 2.

Keep the focus of the question firmly in mind. You are looking to select and comment on parts of the text that convey 'the difference between the doctor and his wife'. As this question is worth 2 marks and it asks about 'the difference between the doctor and his wife', for full marks it is essential that you deal with how both characters are depicted in order to show the difference, i.e. comment on how the doctor is portrayed and then make a separate comment on how his wife is portrayed.

You could consider the following possibilities:

The doctor's wife:
- 'in black' suggests dreariness, sadness and a lack of colour
- 'prophetic dejection' suggests hopelessness and despair for the future, a lack of faith
- 'knocked on it and waited' – her behaviour mirrors that of a servant, suggesting she is a meek and submissive character

The doctor:
- 'effervescent' suggests having lots of energy, brimming over with life, bouncy
- 'as if...he had just discovered a panacea' – a 'panacea' is a cure for all ills. This simile is used to highlight the doctor's happy and upbeat personality, as any doctor who had found a universal cure would be extremely happy

- 'snatched' has connotations of being greedy or selfish
- 'dandle' suggests playfulness, good-natured

Sample answer

The contrast between the doctor and his wife is shown by:

The doctor: 'effervescent' suggests something fizzing with energy and bubbling over, so we see that the doctor is an energetic character who is full of life (1).

The doctor's wife: 'prophetic dejection' suggests that the doctor's wife has an ability to see only bad things in the future and that she is an unhappy and pessimistic person (1).

This answer would gain full marks. The candidate has selected two appropriate quotations/references — one for each character to show the 'difference' — and makes appropriate comments on how each reference conveys an aspect of the different characters' personalities.

Answering the 10-mark question

The 10-mark question is an opportunity to demonstrate your wider knowledge of the text and to show that you can link the extract with the entire novel. Half of the total marks for Scottish text are taken up by this question — a substantial part of the total for the Critical Reading paper — and having a clear understanding of what you need to do in order to meet the question's requirements is essential.

First, it is important that you are aware of how the question is marked. The marks for this question are allocated as follows:

- 2 marks are given for identifying elements of '**commonality**'
- 2 marks are given for discussing the focus of the question **within the extract**
- 6 marks are given for discussing the focus of the question **elsewhere in the novel**

Tackling the sample question

Let's take a closer look at the 10-mark question for the above extract:

> 4 By referring to this extract and to elsewhere in the novel, discuss how Jenkins explores the theme of isolation. (10 marks)

Identifying elements of 'commonality'

'Commonality' is actually provided for you in the question's focus. The 10-mark question will ask you to consider some aspect of the text, for example a theme such as love or isolation; the role of a specific character;

the use of a language feature such as symbolism; or contrast. This aspect of the text — the 'focus' of the question — is 'commonality'. However, there are no marks awarded for simply restating the question's focus; what you have to do is identify 'elements of commonality' and this means that you should take a broad view of the text and identify *what* you have learned about that focus or identify *how* the focus is explored.

It is clear that the focus or 'commonality' of this question is 'the theme of isolation'. You should aim to answer this part of the question by stating *how* your overall understanding of 'isolation' has been developed by the novel or by stating *what* the novel has taught you about 'isolation'.

Sample paragraph

Jenkins explores the theme of isolation by presenting it as a negative force (1) in the lives of several of the novel's characters. Isolation can lead to deep despair and frustration (1), which can disrupt normal lives and relationships, as seen in Duror's life.

In this first part on 'commonality', the candidate has pointed out what the novel reveals about isolation: that it is 'a negative force' that 'can lead to deep despair and frustration', and it 'can disrupt normal lives and relationships'. The candidate also adds that Jenkins uses Duror's life to show the negative effects of isolation. This answer certainly identifies several elements of 'commonality' — the candidate shows how the novel has developed an understanding of 'isolation' by identifying it as a negative force and then noting its devastating consequences. This is a successful answer that would fulfil the requirements of this part of the question.

Discussing the focus of the question within the extract

The 2 marks in this part of the question are awarded for discussing how the focus is shown within the extract. You can answer this question by making a detailed comment on how 'isolation' is shown in the extract or by making two more basic comments on how it is shown in the extract. It is important to remember that, unlike National 5, you will not be awarded marks for simply quoting or referring to examples of isolation; you should always comment on how your chosen quotations/references are used to show the focus of the question.

Sample paragraphs

- *'...stars, so remote, and so oblivious of his infinitely petty existence...' On looking at the stars, Duror realises that he is only a tiny part of the universe and feels that he is insignificant, suggesting his isolation from the world around him (1).*
- *'...he thought that perhaps the old man might be able to prescribe some powder or pills to induce not sleep only but an awakening into a life...' Although Duror has little hope of help*

from the doctor, he wonders briefly if the doctor could prescribe something that will allow him to lead a 'life' again, showing that he feels his life has died in some way and that he is isolated from normal life (1).

The candidate has selected two relevant quotations/references that convey the 'isolation' of a main character (Duror) within the extract. Without comment, these quotations would not gain marks at Higher level, but the candidate makes appropriate comments on each quotation, discussing how Duror's detachment from the world around him is shown. This is a successful answer that fulfils the requirements of this part of the question.

Exam tip
Bullet points have been used for answering here, but it is also acceptable to answer using sentences/ paragraphs.

Discussing the focus of the question elsewhere in the novel

Although this part of the question requires you to take a similar approach to the one taken for the extract, it is important to remember that this is a bigger part of the question – one in which you should demonstrate your knowledge and understanding of the entire text. There are 6 marks available for this part of the question and this is why it is important that you have a thorough knowledge of the novel. You are being asked to dip into your overall knowledge of *The Cone-Gatherers* in order to select appropriate quotations/references and to then comment on how these references relate to the focus of the question. This may seem a daunting task, but you should remember that, as the novel is a substantial piece of literature, you are not expected to quote directly from memory: you may remember and then comment on a quotation that links well with the focus of the question, but it is also perfectly acceptable to use your own words when explaining or referring to a relevant aspect of the text.

Again, there are different ways in which you could approach this part of the question: you could make six basic comments discussing where you think the theme of isolation is explored elsewhere in the novel, you could make three more detailed comments showing where this theme is explored, or you could make a combination of these, to add up to six.

Sample paragraphs

Calum and Neil are isolated as a result of Calum's disability. At times, people can be cruel to Calum because of his appearance. For example, the children in Lendrick tease him and this means that the brothers are happier living an isolated life in the woods of Ardmore.

Peggy is isolated not only through her paralysis but also because Duror is repelled by her physical condition. Because Peggy cannot walk, she has grown 'monstrously obese' and this isolates her even more, as her ageing mother struggles to move her and she is restricted to her room almost all of the time. This means that she has little human contact and, when Duror becomes ever-more reluctant to spend time with her, she becomes depressed.

Jenkins also uses the novel's setting to show how isolation can affect people. The villagers in Lendrick all know each other and it is difficult to keep things private. For example, everyone in the hotel bar knows about Peggy but they don't talk to Duror about this, showing they are willing to gossip in this isolated setting. This can also be seen in the bar when one of the local men gossips about Calum and Neil: 'I hear their mither did away with herself soon after the wee one was born.'

Lady Runcie-Campbell is also isolated because of the setting of wartime, as her husband is on active service. This isolation affects her emotionally, but she also struggles with the added burden of managing the estate in her husband's absence and this causes conflict with her Christian views.

Duror is perhaps the most isolated character. He meets few people in his work as a gamekeeper and his wife's disability has caused him to withdraw into himself. This leads to him becoming frustrated and to his deteriorating mental health.

The candidate has selected five relevant references (one of which has an accompanying quotation) from various parts of the novel and has commented on how these explore the theme of 'isolation'. All of these points would gain marks at Higher level; indeed, some of the comments are 'detailed' and would be worth 2 marks. This is a successful answer that fulfils the requirements of this part of the question. Full sentences/paragraphs have been used for answering here, but it is also acceptable to answer using bullet points.

Setting out your answer

As you have seen, you can answer the 10-mark question using sentences within a mini-essay format or using bullet points. There is no 'right' or 'wrong' way of setting out your answer. However, it may help you to clarify exactly what you wish to say in each section if you structure your answer using headings that reflect how it will be marked, such as Commonality, Extract and Elsewhere.

4.2 Critical Reading Section 2: Critical essay

Target your thinking

- How are critical essay questions structured?
- What topics could you be asked about?
- Why is it important to write a clear introduction?
- How can planning help you to produce a well-structured essay?
- What is the most effective way to use quotations and textual references?

Introduction to the essay

Section 2 of the Critical Reading paper requires you to write a critical essay. A total of 20 marks is available for this section. This is 50% of the Critical Reading paper and 20% of your overall mark.

> **Exam tip**
>
> Remember that you can write a Section 2 critical essay on *The Cone-Gatherers* only if you have studied a second writer or text (not prose) from the SQA Scottish text list and used that one for your Scottish text in Section 1. *You must not answer both the Scottish text and critical essay sections on the same novel or the same genre.*

There is no specified order in which you have to complete the sections, although most candidates prefer to answer the Scottish text questions before completing the critical essay. You should ensure that you allocate an appropriate amount of time to each section. Remember that you have 1 hour and 30 minutes for the whole paper, so you should allow approximately 45 minutes for the completion of each section.

Before you even begin to practise writing critical essays, it is important that you know the text really well and have a clear understanding of what is involved in choosing a suitable question for your text. As this study guide is focused on *The Cone-Gatherers*, detailed consideration will be given to **prose** questions. However, many of the general points made about the structure of critical essay questions, how to choose a suitable question and planning/organising your essay will also be useful when you are writing essays on other texts or different genres.

> **Glossary**
>
> **prose:** this is the 'ordinary' form of written or spoken language, one in which the language has no poetic structure and flows naturally without poetic techniques such as rhythm or rhyme. In literature, prose is normally associated with novels, short stories, essays and journalism.

The first thing you will notice about the critical essay questions (for National 5 and Higher) is that they are all composed of two sentences. These two sentences are designed to guide you to the question that best suits your knowledge and understanding of *The Cone-Gatherers*. Obviously, the questions will vary from year to year and Higher questions are more complex than those at National 5. However, the key 'features' of the novel – such as a theme, a significant incident, an important character, a setting or a specific technique – are all topics that you are likely to encounter in the questions. In fact, most of these features are listed in the guidance box provided just before the Prose questions (similar guidance boxes are provided before the questions for each genre). Having a good knowledge and understanding of such features in the novel is therefore important if you wish to produce an essay that will do well.

The first sentence of each essay question will immediately tell you whether your text – *The Cone-Gatherers* – could be used to answer the essay task contained in the second sentence. When you have looked at the first sentences for each question, you will be able to judge if the questions are likely to be suitable for *The Cone-Gatherers*. You will also be able to make an initial judgement on which question has the better 'focus' for your knowledge of the novel.

When you have considered all of the first sentences, you then need to look at the second sentence for each question that matches your text. *The second sentence is important as it tells you exactly what you have to do in your essay.* When you have read these task sentences, you will have to decide which question fits best with your knowledge of the text. You can then start planning your essay.

The next sections of the book provide useful advice on planning and writing your critical essay. As *The Cone-Gatherers* is a 'crossover' text – an option at National 5 and Higher – the sections are sub-divided with advice for each level.

> If you are studying at National 5, read the information below. If you are studying at Higher level, turn to page 95.

Advice for National 5

You should look at the Prose section if you decide to write your critical essay on *The Cone-Gatherers*. There are two essay questions for each genre in the National 5 Critical Reading paper. You should look at Questions 3 and 4 as these are the questions for Prose.

The following questions are similar to those found in a National 5 Prose section.

Exam tip

Answers to questions in this part should refer to the text and to such relevant features as characterisation, setting, language, key incident(s), climax, turning point, plot, structure, narrative technique, theme, ideas, description…

3 Choose a novel or short story or work of non-fiction which explores a theme in an interesting way.

By referring to appropriate techniques, explain how the author explores the theme in an interesting way.

4 Choose a novel or short story or work of non-fiction in which there is a character for whom you feel sympathy.

By referring to appropriate techniques, show how the author makes you feel sympathy for this character.

Just as for the Scottish text in Section 1, you should be able to 'decode' these questions and identify the focus in order to help you choose the question that is most suitable for your knowledge of the text.

You might want to think about the following process when making the final choice for your essay question:

Q3 The focus is *'a novel…which explores a theme in an interesting way'*. Do you think *The Cone-Gatherers* contains a theme which Jenkins explores in an interesting way?

You might think…

Yes, the novel deals with the theme of good and evil. Jenkins uses a variety of interesting characters and a series of interesting events to explore this theme. So, this question would work well with *The Cone-Gatherers*.

Q4 The focus is *'a novel…in which there is a character for whom you feel sympathy'*. Did you feel sympathy for any of the characters in the novel?

You might think…

Yes, there are quite a few characters who fit this description. Calum and Neil have difficult lives throughout the novel. Duror is not a pleasant character, but he has suffered as a result of Peggy's illness and his frustrated life, and his mental health deteriorates throughout the novel. Lady Runcie-Campbell is also an option as she struggles with the burden of running the estate and the conflict this causes between her social class and her Christian values. So, this question would work well with *The Cone-Gatherers*.

However, you need to choose only *one* character to consider in your essay, so you need to make this choice based on the character you think is the best 'match'.

In fact, *The Cone-Gatherers* is likely to be a good 'match' with many questions. It is a text:

- with strong characters
- with powerful themes
- containing significant incidents such as the deer drive and the storm/beach hut
- that has a vivid setting
- with a memorable ending
- that uses the feature of symbolism throughout

When you have considered all of the first sentences, you then need to look at the second sentence for each question that matches your text. *The second sentence is important as it tells you exactly what you have to do in your essay.* When you have read these task sentences, you will have to decide which question fits best with your knowledge of the text. You can then start planning your essay.

The following sections look at planning, the importance of writing a clear introduction, structuring a line of thought, using quotations/references to support your points and writing a conclusion. Although both questions above would work well, Question 3 will be used here.

Tackling a sample question

> 3   Choose a novel or short story or work of non-fiction which explores a theme in an interesting way.
>
> By referring to appropriate techniques, explain how the author explores the theme in an interesting way.

Planning your essay

It is always a good idea to make a rough plan of what you would like to include in your essay before you start writing. Creating a plan takes only a few minutes and will help you to:

- focus on the question and keep a relevant line of thought throughout your essay
- decide on the different parts of the novel/quotations you wish to include in your analysis and evaluation of the novel
- create a logical structure for your thoughts

Plans come in all shapes and sizes. You could plan by writing a few simple notes or headings, or you could plan in a more 'visual' way by using a mind-map or a flow chart. Trying out some of these different planning methods when writing practice/revision essays will help you decide what kind of plan works best for you.

A simple plan for Question 3 could be written in a flow chart like this:

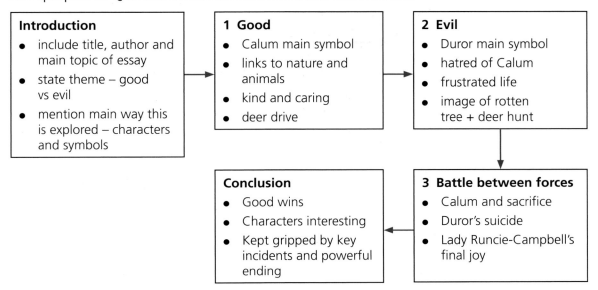

Introduction
- include title, author and main topic of essay
- state theme – good vs evil
- mention main way this is explored – characters and symbols

1 Good
- Calum main symbol
- links to nature and animals
- kind and caring
- deer drive

2 Evil
- Duror main symbol
- hatred of Calum
- frustrated life
- image of rotten tree + deer hunt

3 Battle between forces
- Calum and sacrifice
- Duror's suicide
- Lady Runcie-Campbell's final joy

Conclusion
- Good wins
- Characters interesting
- Kept gripped by key incidents and powerful ending

Alternatively, the content in this flow chart could just be set down as simple bullet points under headings.

Writing an introduction

Your introduction should give the marker a clear idea of your main line of thought. The marker should be able to tell what question you are answering and the main ideas you will focus on from reading this introduction (make sure you also write the question number in the margin). The very best essays have a line of thought that is 'consistently relevant' and writing a clear introduction can help you to achieve this. If you explain what you intend to do in your essay, you will also be able to look back at your introduction and stay on the right track with your ideas.

Sample introduction

In his novel 'The Cone-Gatherers', Robin Jenkins explores the ongoing battle between good and evil in an interesting way. The book is set in wartime when the forces of good and evil were in conflict. The two sides of this battle are represented in the novel by characters who have completely opposite natures. The characters work on an estate in the peaceful Scottish Highlands. Calum is an innocent disabled man who gathers cones with his brother Neil. Jenkins presents Calum as the symbol for good. Duror, a gamekeeper with an unhappy life, is the symbol for evil. The conflict between them is interesting as it ends in tragedy, but good triumphs in the end.

This introduction shows straight away that the candidate has a 'good understanding' of the themes (mentions good and evil and the war); is 'familiar' with the setting and characters (refers to wartime, Scottish Highlands, Duror and Calum); and has an 'awareness of techniques' (mentions symbol and conflict). There is also a clear reference to the question at the beginning and at the end of the introduction, and the mention of the characters sets up the essay's structure.

In terms of language and expression, this paragraph 'communicates the line of thought clearly'. There are no errors in spelling, grammar or sentencing/punctuation so expression is 'consistently accurate' so far. Your essay does not have to be perfect – some slips are allowed – but the very best essays are 'consistently accurate'.

Structuring your essay

Your essay should have a clear line of thought and there should be an overall flow in your ideas. Keeping the following points in mind will help you to do this:

- 'familiarity with the text' – your knowledge and understanding of the novel
- 'relevance of line of thought' – how closely you focus on the essay question/task
- 'analysis of the text' – your awareness of the writer's use of literary techniques
- 'evaluation of the text' – how well you have personally responded to the text
- 'accuracy' – how well you express your thoughts

Writing a conclusion

The conclusion to your essay should be quite short. It is a good idea to remind the marker of the focus of your essay. You can use key words from the question's focus to do this, in this case 'theme' and 'interesting'. You should not include any new ideas or repeat what you have already said, but you could sum up the ideas in your line of thought very briefly. The best conclusions join naturally to the essay's line of thought – perhaps summing up your understanding of a theme, a character or a technique used by the writer.

Sample essay

The following essay uses the flow chart plan given for Question 3 and would join with the introductory paragraph given earlier.

1 Use of topic sentence helps to maintain relevance and to structure the line of thought.

2 Appropriate quotation – placed after a colon as evidence to support the point being made.

4 Use of topic sentence helps to maintain relevance and to structure the line of thought.

5 Appropriate quotation/ reference skilfully integrated with sentence/ideas.

7 Use of topic sentence helps to maintain relevance and to structure the line of thought.

8 Appropriate quotation/ reference skilfully integrated with sentence/ideas.

One of the main reasons I found the novel interesting was because of the memorable characters. Calum is used to show the theme of good and he is a very unusual character. Calum and Neil have been sent to the Lendrickmore estate to gather cones to replace the trees cut down for the war effort. Calum is disabled as he is physically deformed. He looks unattractive but has a beautiful face. In the trees, he is described as being 'as agile as a monkey'. He is happy in his total innocence and his enjoyment of nature. He loves all animals and would not harm anything: 'This was the terrifying mystery, why creatures he loved should kill one another.' Calum's kindness sets him up as the symbol of 'good', but his presence in the woods disturbs the gamekeeper, Duror.

Duror is another interesting character used to explore the theme of good and evil. When Neil and Calum come to the woods, Duror is already struggling with an unhappy life. His wife, Peggy, is paralysed and has grown 'monstrously obese' and Duror is now too old to enlist for war although he wants to fight. Jenkins lets us know that Duror is directly opposed to Calum because, the first time we see him, he is 'aiming his gun' at Calum. The good-hearted Calum is upset because a rabbit is injured in one of Duror's snares. As Duror watches Calum, he is described as being in an 'icy sweat of hatred'. The image here shows Duror's cold nature and malice.

Although Calum is too simple to understand Duror's hatred, he senses it. By making these characters opposites, Jenkins begins to show the battle between good and evil. Duror's deteriorating mental condition is partly triggered by Calum's arrival. Jenkins lets us see Duror's thoughts and we learn that he 'is repelled by anything living that had an imperfection or deformity'. In some ways, Calum seems to remind him of his wife, Peggy, who is now deformed

3 Analysis shows a good awareness of writer's techniques/features in terms of the essay question.

6 Analysis shows a good awareness of writer's techniques/features in terms of the essay question.

through illness. The woods were Duror's 'sanctuary' from his unhappy life but, with Calum there, he feels they have been polluted. With nowhere to escape, Duror gradually grows more and more evil. Jenkins uses the symbol of a dying tree to show Duror's deterioration.

One of the other interesting ways Jenkins explores this theme is by showing Duror manipulating events. He lies to the Lady of the estate to force Calum into a deer drive, hoping Calum will be killed or removed from the woods. This is a key incident, as Duror's plan does not work. Calum tries to save a deer, but Duror is overcome by his hatred and cuts the deer's throat in a frenzy while thinking of Peggy. The hunting party do not understand his confusion and Calum is blamed for spoiling the hunt.

Calum gets to stay in the woods and Duror is even more frustrated, so he ends up believing that Calum must die: 'his going therefore must be a destruction, an agony, a crucifixion.' This leads to the final clash where the innocent Calum is sacrificed by Duror. Duror learns of Neil's refusal to help rescue Lady Runcie-Campbell's son and sees this as an excuse to go after Calum. Good and evil clash, with the good and innocent Calum gathering cones while Duror shoots him. To try to rid himself of his frustrations, Duror — totally evil by now — kills Calum because Calum's deformity has become a symbol of Duror's deformed life. Duror finds no release in the murder and takes his own life.

The theme is made even more interesting because, although Calum dies, evil does not win. Duror is described as walking away with 'so infinite a desolation' after Calum's murder, whereas Calum is still smiling. Calum's blood dripping to earth also causes Lady Runcie-Campbell to see that his death was the sacrifice needed to rid the woods of evil in the person of Duror.

11 Appropriate quotation/reference skilfully integrated with sentence/ideas.

13 Analysis shows a good awareness of writer's techniques/features in terms of the essay question.

15 Appropriate quotation/reference skilfully integrated with sentence/ideas.

9 Analysis shows a good awareness of writer's techniques/features in terms of the essay question.

10 Use of topic sentence helps to maintain relevance and to structure the line of thought.

12 Appropriate quotation – placed after a colon as evidence to support the point being made.

14 Use of topic sentence helps to maintain relevance and to structure the line of thought.

This essay would achieve a high mark as it is relevant to the question throughout. It includes appropriate references and/or quotations to support the line of thought and analytical/evaluative comments. It is also well written with no errors in spelling, punctuation or expression. Look closely at how the references and quotations are used. The strongest essays tend to merge quotations with the points being made. It is also possible to use quotation as evidence by inserting it after a colon following the point being made. There are also references to the key incident of the deer drive and the ending. The words 'symbol' and 'imagery' also show an awareness of the writer's techniques.

Advice for Higher

You should look at the Prose – Fiction section if you decide to write your critical essay on *The Cone-Gatherers*. There are three essay questions for each genre in the Higher Critical Reading paper. You should look at Questions 4, 5 and 6 as these are the question numbers for Prose – Fiction.

The following questions are similar to those found in a Higher Prose section.

> **Exam tip**
>
> Answers to questions on prose fiction should refer to the text and to such relevant features as characterisation, setting, language, key incident(s), climax, turning point, plot, structure, narrative technique, theme, ideas, description.

4   Choose a novel or short story which features a character who experiences feelings of hatred or bitterness or anger.

With reference to appropriate techniques, explain how the author makes you aware of the character's feelings and discuss how this aspect of the character adds to your appreciation of the text as a whole.

5   Choose a novel or short story in which there is a shocking or uplifting incident.

With reference to appropriate techniques, explain briefly the shocking or uplifting nature of this incident and discuss how the incident adds to your appreciation of the text as a whole.

6   Choose a novel or short story which is notable for its effective use of symbolism or setting.

With reference to appropriate techniques, explain how this feature is used effectively and discuss how its use contributes to your appreciation of the text as a whole.

Just as for Scottish text in Section 1, these questions can be 'decoded' to offer you useful guidance. The first sentence will immediately tell you whether your text – *The Cone-Gatherers* – could be used to answer the actual essay task contained in the second sentence. When you have looked at the first sentences for each question, you will be able to judge if the questions 'match' the novel. You will also be able to make an initial judgement on which question has the better focus for your knowledge of the novel.

You might want to think about the following process when making the final choice for your essay question:

Q4 The focus is 'a novel…which features a character who experiences feelings of hatred **or** bitterness **or** anger'. Do you think *The Cone-Gatherers* features a character who experiences any one of these feelings (notice that 'or' is repeated, which means that your chosen character needs to experience only one of these emotions)?

You might think…

Yes, Jenkins uses a variety of characters who experience these emotions. Duror experiences all of them; Neil experiences bitterness and anger. So, this question is likely to be a good 'match' for *The Cone-Gatherers*.

Q5 The focus is 'a novel…in which there is a shocking **or** uplifting incident'. Do you think that any of the incidents in the novel fit this description?

You might think…

Yes, although 'shocking' would be a better choice than 'uplifting' when writing an essay for this question. Roderick's desire to give the cone-gatherers a lift in the car and Lady Runcie-Campbell's new awareness at the conclusion of the novel could be viewed as 'uplifting'. However, there are several key incidents in the novel that could be viewed as 'shocking' – most notably the deer drive, Neil and Calum's expulsion from the beach hut, and the horrific climax of Calum's murder and Duror's suicide. These 'shocking' incidents offer greater scope for writing a critical essay on the novel. So, this question is also likely to be a good 'match'.

Q6 The focus is 'a novel…which is notable for its effective use of symbolism or setting'. Both of these features are used effectively in *The Cone-Gatherers*. However, Jenkins' use of symbolism is highly significant throughout the text, so this would be a better choice for an essay.

You might think…

Yes, symbolism is used in a variety of ways. For example, Calum and Duror are symbols of good and evil respectively; Lady Runcie-Campbell symbolises the fixed views of an older upper class whereas Roderick symbolises a less rigid future class order; Duror is symbolised by the repeated image of the decaying tree. So, this question could also work well.

When you have considered all of the first sentences, you then need to look at the second sentence for each question that matches your text. *The second sentence is important as it tells you exactly what you have to do in your essay.* When you have read these task sentences, you will have to decide which question fits best with your knowledge of the text. You can then start planning your essay.

The following sections look at planning your essay, writing a clear introduction, structuring a line of thought and writing a conclusion. You should also use references/quotations to support the points you make in the main body of your essay. Although all three questions above would work well, Question 4 will be used here.

Tackling a sample question

4 Choose a novel or short story which features a character who experiences feelings of hatred or bitterness or anger.

With reference to appropriate techniques, explain how the author makes you aware of the character's feelings and discuss how this aspect of the character adds to your appreciation of the text as a whole.

Planning your essay

It is always a good idea to make a rough plan of what you would like to include in your essay before you start writing. Creating a plan takes only a few minutes and will help you to:

- focus on the question and keep a relevant line of thought throughout your essay
- decide on the different parts of the novel/quotations you wish to include in your analysis and evaluation of the novel
- create a logical structure for your thoughts

Plans come in all shapes and sizes. You could plan by writing a few simple notes or headings, or you could plan in a more 'visual' way by using a mind-map or a flow chart. An example of a flow chart plan for a National 5 critical essay is given on page 91. Trying out some of these different planning methods when writing practice/revision essays will help you decide what kind of plan works best for you.

Before you write your plan, you need to look at exactly what you are asked to do. In this case, you first need to decide on the character and the feeling you will write about in your essay. That should be straightforward. As already noted, there are several options you could choose, but the most obvious choice would be Duror's hatred for Calum.

The actual task asks you to 'explain how' Jenkins presents this feeling – in other words, write about where we see Duror's hatred and the effect this has on him and other characters. The question also asks you to 'discuss how' Duror's hatred 'adds to your appreciation of the text as a whole'. You will see that this phrase – or very similar phrasing - is commonly used in Higher critical essay questions. Put very simply, it means that you should explain how the focus of the question has developed your understanding of the wider text. For example, in an essay on Question 4 you might want to comment on how Duror's hatred highlights the themes of good and evil, or you could comment on how it has deepened your understanding of his character or an aspect of human nature.

A quick and simple plan could then be written using headings like this:

Duror – feelings of hatred

Intro – title, author, identify Duror and give background/setting for him, explain hatred is for Calum, link to themes/battle between good and evil

Duror at start of novel – watching Calum with gun aimed, invading his sanctuary in woods, difficult life at home, hatred taking him over and evil growing

Hatred causes Duror to manipulate people/deteriorate – Lady R-C, key incident deer drive and hallucinates about Peggy, evil causes deterioration in his physical and mental health, lies about the doll and decides to kill Calum

Calum remains good but will be a sacrifice to get rid of Duror's evil. Duror becomes more twisted – Lady R-C and Tulloch realise something is wrong but not quick enough to stop tragedy. Duror desolate – suicide ends evil and Calum's death brings hope

Writing an introduction

Introductions are important. The marker should be able to tell what question you are answering from reading your introduction, so it is often a good idea to refer directly to the question when you are identifying the text and the author. Your introduction should give the marker a clear idea of your main line of thought, so referring to your plan will allow you to tell the marker (in a few short sentences) what you intend to consider in your essay. You should also aim to give a sense of your overall grasp of the novel in terms of the question. Good critical essays should sound like a natural response to the question, so it is important to avoid phrases such as 'In this essay I am going to write about…'. Instead of using a mechanical phrase, you could simply start with a first sentence that refers to the words of the question. For example:

Sample introduction

In 'The Cone-Gatherers' by Robin Jenkins, John Duror is a character who is consumed by an irrational hatred that eventually leads him to commit murder before taking his own life...

This first sentence lets the marker know which text you will be considering and which question you will be addressing. After the first sentence, you could incorporate some of the other details noted in the first points of your plan. It is also a good idea to mention the theme briefly (and naturally) in your introduction as this will then allow you to make comments throughout your essay showing your 'appreciation of the text as a whole'.

Structuring your essay

Your essay should have a clear line of thought throughout. In other words, your ideas should follow a logical flow rather than just being a series of disjointed points. Keeping the following points in mind will help you to do this:

- 'knowledge and understanding' – examines how well you know the text/understand its themes/character/plot and how appropriately you select evidence to support your points
- 'focus on the demands of the question' – examines the relevance of your essay in terms of the question
- 'analysis' – examines how well you can comment on the writer's use of literary techniques and their effects
- 'evaluation' – examines the extent of your engagement with the text
- 'technical accuracy' – examines technical features such as spelling, grammar and sentencing

Writing a conclusion

The conclusion to your essay should be fairly succinct. It is a good idea to remind the marker of the main focus of your essay by using some key words from the question's focus, in this case the character's 'hatred'. You should not introduce any new ideas or repeat details of what you have already said, but you may wish to summarise your main line of thought very briefly. It is also a good idea to avoid using a mechanical first sentence in your concluding paragraph; phrases such as 'In conclusion...' or 'To conclude...' can seem artificial. It is a better idea to bring your line of thought to a natural conclusion that is linked to the focus of the question – for example, an overarching statement on character, feature or theme.

Sample essay

The following essay uses the above plan for Question 4.

In 'The Cone-Gatherers' by Robin Jenkins, John Duror is a character who is consumed by an irrational hatred that eventually leads him to commit murder before taking his own life. The novel is set during the Second World War, when Duror is a gamekeeper on the Lendrickmore Estate in Argyll. The estate is owned by the aristocratic Runcie-Campbell family and Duror is able to spread his hatred and cause evil on the estate because Lady Runcie-Campbell often looks to him for advice in the absence of her husband. Jenkins presents Duror as a character who is filled with hatred in order to establish him as a symbol for evil: one of the novel's main themes is the ongoing battle between good and evil.

At the start of the novel, Jenkins makes us aware of Duror's feelings by first introducing us to the cone-gathering brothers, Neil and Calum McPhie. These men are gathering cones as a wartime duty, and Calum is depicted as a good and caring character. Within the first chapter, we see Calum happily working in the trees with the birds who are his friends: 'chaffinches fluttered round him…now and then one would alight on his head'. Calum, with a deformed body but a face which is 'beautiful with trust', is a clear symbol for good. In contrast, when we see Duror for the first time, his hatred for Calum is made clear: he is described as having 'his gun aimed all the time at the feebleminded hunchback'. Duror's hatred is all the more shocking because we have already seen Calum's goodness, so the symbolic nature of these characters is established early.

1 Use of topic sentence helps to maintain relevance and to structure the line of thought.

2 Appropriate quotation – placed after a colon as evidence to support the point being made.

3 Analysis shows a good awareness of writer's techniques/features in terms of the essay question.

4 Use of topic sentence helps to maintain relevance and to structure the line of thought.

Jenkins quickly reveals why Duror hates Calum so much. Until the arrival of Neil and Calum, the woods were Duror's 'stronghold and sanctuary' – a place he could go to 'fortify his sanity and hope'. He needs the woods to escape the miseries of his life. For the past 18 years, his wife has been bedridden, having suffered an accident only a few years after their marriage. As Duror cannot stand anything that has an 'imperfection or deformity', he is repulsed by his wife and frustrated in his loveless marriage. He is also frustrated because he has tried to enlist for service three times but has been refused because he is too old. Calum becomes the focus for all of Duror's frustrations and hatred because his deformity seems to Duror to be a reflection of his own miserable life. Jenkins describes Duror's dark thoughts: 'For many years his life had been stunted, misshapen…this misbegotten creature was its personification' and we see that evil begins to flourish from this hatred.

5 Appropriate quotation/ reference skilfully integrated with sentence/ideas.

6 Analysis shows a good awareness of writer's techniques/features in terms of the essay question.

7 Appropriate quotation – placed after a colon as evidence to support the point being made.

8 Analysis shows a good awareness of writer's techniques/features in terms of the essay question.

Duror's mental and physical health quickly deteriorates. Determined to get rid of Calum, he lies to Lady Runcie-Campbell in order to force the animal-loving Calum into beating for a deer hunt. Duror knows the brothers have no power to refuse and he even lies about the innocent Calum, accusing him of obscene acts. Duror's willingness to lie makes him seem like a demonic presence in the woods. We see his deterioration when, before the deer hunt, he dreams that his wife is being pecked to death by thrushes.

9 Use of topic sentence helps to maintain relevance and to structure the line of thought.

The deer hunt is a key incident in the novel because it is the point of no return for Duror's deterioration. When Calum tries to save a deer, throwing himself on to the wounded animal to comfort it, Jenkins describes Duror's 'furious force' as he 'savagely' cuts the deer's throat. Duror then asks for his wife and it is clear that he seems to have associated killing the deer with

10 Appropriate quotation/reference skilfully integrated with sentence/ideas.

killing Peggy. When he recovers and realises what has happened, he directs all of his hatred into getting rid of the innocent Calum. In the battle between good and evil, Duror seems the stronger force at this point. Yet Duror deteriorates further, spreading obscene rumours about Calum, mumbling horrible lies to the Lady and other characters. Even his physical appearance degenerates and he is 'unkempt with the neck of his shirt grubby…boots thick with mud…his hair was so much whiter'. It seems as if Duror begins to lose his own battle with evil as he is caught up in his sick lies about Calum and his plot to get rid of the brothers.

Only close to the final tragedy do some of the other characters see the hatred and evil that lurk within Duror. Lady Runcie-Campbell's Christian faith is challenged by her last speech with Duror, as she realises something is wrong with him but sends him away in disgust instead of trying to intervene. When she learns that Duror is on his way to look for Neil and Calum after they refuse to help her son climb down from the tree, it is clear that she knows what may happen – and that evil may win over goodness.

Jenkins describes her regret for her harsh treatment of the humble cone-gatherers. She hears the shot that kills Calum, but she also sees a 'desolate' Duror walking away to take his own life. Duror's hatred, and the battle between good and evil, end with the final tragedy, but Jenkins makes it clear that hatred and evil have not been triumphant. He uses a final symbol of the cones and Calum's blood falling to earth, almost like seeds and suggesting regeneration. Even Calum's death is symbolised as being like a 'crucifixion' – also suggesting new life and hope. This is what Lady Runcie-Campbell recognises when she weeps 'on her knees' beside the blood and cones.

This essay would achieve a high mark as it shows a secure knowledge and understanding of the text. It has detailed textual evidence to support the line of thought and the analysis of Jenkins' use of characterisation, key incident and symbolism is detailed. There are no issues with technical accuracy. Look closely at how the references and quotations have often been integrated into the candidate's sentences – the strongest essays tend to merge quotations with the points being made. It is possible to use a quotation as evidence by inserting it after a colon following the point being made, which is done several times in this essay.

Both parts of the Critical Reading paper are 'closed book', meaning that you are not allowed to consult the novel during the exam. Answering the Scottish text questions and writing a critical essay requires you to demonstrate a knowledge of the text as a whole. Whether you opt to use *The Cone-Gatherers* for writing your critical essay or for answering the Scottish text questions, you will need to use textual references or quotations to support your points. Although it is acceptable to refer to specific parts of the text without the use of quotations to support your points, you may find it helpful to familiarise yourself with the quotations given here. These have been organised into groups for 'character' and 'theme'. However, it is important to remember that these groupings are not rigid. Ultimately, your decision to use a particular quotation will depend entirely on the point you are making.

Quotations for character

Calum

1 'This was the terrifying mystery, why creatures he loved should kill one another.'

- Reveals Calum's compassion for other creatures and his lack of understanding of nature's cruelty.

2 'Calum no longer was one of the beaters; he too was a deer hunted by remorseless men.'

- Reveals Calum's distress and concern for the deer during the hunt, and his close connection with animals.

3 'He hung therefore in twisted fashion, and kept swinging. His arms were loose and dangled in macabre gestures of supplication. Though he smiled he was dead.'

- Calum is left hanging in the tree, caught by the strap of his cone bag, after Duror has shot him. Jenkins' description of Calum's position in the tree is suggestive of crucifixion and this emphasises the key idea that Calum has been a sacrifice that banishes the evil brought by Duror.

Duror

'Hidden among the spruces...stood Duror the gamekeeper, in an icy sweat of hatred, with his gun aimed all the time at the feebleminded hunchback grovelling over the rabbit.'

4

- In the very early pages of the novel, Duror's hatred of Calum is made clear.

'Since childhood Duror had been repelled by anything living that had an imperfection or deformity or lack...'

5

- Reveals Duror's pathological aversion to deformity; another reason for his hatred of Calum.

'He was like a tree still straight, still showing green leaves; but underground death was creeping along the roots.'

6

- Jenkins frequently uses the image of a dying tree to describe Duror's deteriorating condition.

'He was walking away among the pine trees with so infinite a desolation in his every step...'

7

- After murdering Calum, Duror remains 'desolate' and, finding no hope of release from his misery, takes his own life.

Lady Runcie-Campbell

'To obey Christ by being humble must mean to betray her husband, and also, perhaps, to amuse her equals.'

8

- Reveals the internal conflict Lady Runcie-Campbell faces when she tries to reconcile her duties as an upper-class landowner with her Christian values.

'She could not pray, but she could weep; and as she wept pity, and purified hope, and joy, welled up in her heart.'

9

- Lady Runcie-Campbell's reaction to the humble Calum's death reveals her sudden realisation that evil has been banished and that Calum's death has acted as a sacrifice bringing hope and redemption.

Neil

10 'Another hindrance had been the constant sight of the mansion house chimneys, reminding him of their hut, which to him remained a symbol of humiliation.'

- Neil's bitterness at the inequality caused by the social class system is seen in the anger and frustration he feels whenever he sees the mansion house.

Quotations for theme

Good and evil

1 'Is to be always happy a crime? Is it daft never to be angry or jealous or full of spite? You're better and wiser than any of them.'

- Neil's love for his brother is made clear here, and the description clearly shows Calum's goodness.

2 'He had read that the Germans were putting idiots and cripples to death in gas chambers. Outwardly, as everybody expected, he condemned such barbarity; inwardly...he had profoundly approved.'

- Duror's shocking approval of Nazi atrocities ensures that we see him as a symbol of evil.

3 'His going therefore must be a destruction, an agony, a crucifixion.'

- Duror's thoughts on removing Calum from the woods suggest Calum's suffering will be a symbolic sacrifice.

4 'The truth was, as Neil knew, Calum was too honest, generous and truly meek.'

- Neil thinks about the way in which Calum treats the conscientious objectors with the same kindness he shows to everyone else, even though others treat them cruelly. This meekness further associates Calum with goodness.

5 'Here at the very hut was the most evil presence of all, and it was visible.'

- Roderick watches Duror spying on the cone-gatherers and becomes aware of Duror's malevolent nature.

War

'He remembered that in the war being fought far from there, men were being shot in greater numbers and with bitterer hatred than ever crows were.'

6

- Neil's thoughts reveal the horror and terrible devastation caused by war.

'He had read often in the newspapers and had heard on the wireless that the war was being fought so that ordinary humble people could live in peace without being bullied and enslaved by brutal men with power...'

7

- When Neil thinks of the war, he hopes that it will bring about a more equal world where people like himself and Calum will have a better life.

Social class

'Your father's right. After this war, the lower orders are going to be frightfully presumptuous.'

8

- After sending the cone-gatherers from the beach hut into the storm once again, Lady Runcie-Campbell is unable to take a compassionate view and shows her concern for social superiority.

'It's taken centuries of breeding to produce our kind. For God's sake don't get us mixed.'

9

- When Lady Runcie-Campbell worries about Roderick's friendliness to the servants and the cone-gatherers, she recalls her husband's determination to preserve strict social class barriers.

Religion

'It seems to me a shameful thing, to torment the living unjustly and think to remedy it by pampering the dead.'

10

- Mrs Lochie, although believing in God, finds no comfort in the belief that Peggy's suffering will be rewarded in heaven. Her lack of faith in conventional Christian ideas is in contrast to Lady Runcie-Campbell's acceptance of them.

Answers to the 'Review your learning' sections.

Context (p. 13)

1 Context means how a writer might have been influenced by various outside factors/other works of literature. Where the text sits in relation to literary genres or traditions.

2 He was a conscientious objector and was assigned to forestry operations for wartime service.

3 1939–45.

4 Smaller communities in Britain may have been more remote from direct fighting but were still greatly affected. For example, most able-bodied men of a suitable age would have been away on active service, so staff shortages in many areas were common. Military bases and training camps were often set up in remote areas. Rationing existed everywhere in Britain.

5 Social class structure in Britain at that time was still very rigid.
There was almost no social movement between classes.

6 Symbolism means the use of symbols to represent an idea or a meaning which is not literal.

7 Calum symbolises good, Duror symbolises evil. (You could also refer to other characters who could be viewed as symbolic.)

8 An allegory is a text, usually a story, in which the characters and events take on a much deeper moral, political or religious meaning.

Plot and structure (p. 25)

1 Neil and Calum have not been allowed to stay in the beach hut.

The hut they have been given is tiny and very shoddily made.

2 Duror's wife has been paralysed for 18 years of the couple's 20-year marriage and has become obese. Duror is repelled by her physical condition and is unable to show affection to her. He has tried to enlist in the army three times but has been rejected because of his age. He feels trapped.

3 Duror is described as a diseased and dying tree.

4 Beaters: Neil, Calum, Harry (gardener's apprentice), Betty (land girl), Erchie (handyman), Charlie (Mr Adamson's labourer), Duror
Hunters: Lady Runcie-Campbell, Captain Forgan (her brother),
Mr Adamson, Mr Baird

5 Calum's hobby is woodcarving.

6 Roderick is rescued by Harry.

Characterisation (p. 43)

1 The housekeeper is Mrs Morton.

2 Lady Runcie-Campbell's father was a judge.

3 Sir Colin is concerned about Roderick's kind and friendly manner with servants and others of a lower class. He believes that Roderick is 'over-familiar' and needs to act in accordance with his upper-class background.

4 Peggy is looked after by her mother, Mrs Lochie.

5 When describing Duror's deteriorating mental condition, Jenkins uses the symbols of a dying tree or a 'gale'/storm.

6 Neil wanted to go to sea/work on a ship.

7 Lady Runcie-Campbell.

Themes (p. 57)

1 A theme is an idea or issue that the writer explores in the text.

2 Main themes in *The Cone-Gatherers* are good and evil, social class, war, nature and religion.

3 Characterisation, symbolism, setting and key incidents are some of the techniques/features used by Jenkins to convey the main themes.

4 Good and evil, and the ongoing battle between these forces.

5 Jenkins considers the destructive nature of war, as well as the fact that war can bring change to even the most remote settings.

6 Roderick's more open and accepting attitude to those of a lower class (e.g. Harry and Mrs Morton) is used to suggest that the future, as represented by Roderick's younger generation, may bring a more flexible class structure.

Language features and analysis (p. 67)

1 Jenkins uses many language features in *The Cone-Gatherers*. For example, word choice, imagery, symbolism and pathetic fallacy have been considered in this guide alongside 'wider' features such as characterisation, setting and key incident.

2 Connotation is the idea suggested by a word. This is slightly different from the literal meaning of the word.

3 A metaphor is a comparison in which a writer states – or implies – one thing is another thing, both sides of the comparison sharing a similar quality.

4 Imagery is a language technique in which a writer uses a comparison, usually a simile or metaphor, to represent something. Such comparisons are designed to give us a clearer mental 'picture' or 'image' of the thing being described.

5 The row of silver fir trees that forms a 'fence' between the Runcie-Campbells' mansion and the rest of the estate is used symbolically to represent the rigid social barrier between the upper and lower classes. (You could also refer to the doll, the cones or the decaying tree as symbols from the text.)

6 Pathetic fallacy is a language feature in which the natural world seems to reflect the emotions or events occurring within the text. For example, the weather is often used to create a mood that suits events.

7 The narrative stance used in the novel is of an omniscient third-person narrator.

8 Dialogue is used to convey aspects of character (e.g. social class, emotions) as well as to highlight central concerns.

7 Glossary

allegory: a text, usually a story, in which the characters and events take on a much deeper moral or political or religious meaning

alliteration: the repetition of consonant sounds at the start of words to create a range of impacts and to link ideas together

analyse: to break something down into its constituent parts in order to understand how it is made or how it works. Analysis in literature means to examine a text in detail and gain an understanding of how the writer has used different literary techniques to create an effective piece of work

antagonist: in literature, a person or force that is set against the story's protagonist (often seen as the 'main' character or hero). An antagonist often acts in a hostile or immoral manner

atmosphere: the feelings evoked by the writer through, for example, description of setting

character: a person, animal or figure in a literary work

characterisation: the means by which a writer represents characters in a literary work, i.e. how the writer provides us with information to let us 'see' what a character is like. Characterisation can be direct, where the narrator tells us something about a character, or indirect, where we have to infer something from the character's reactions or actions towards other characters

climax: the point in a narrative when tension or conflict is often at its highest and which comes just before this tension is resolved

colloquialisms: informal words or phrases; slang words

connotations: the ideas suggested by a word; this is slightly different from the literal meaning (or denotation) of the word

conscientious objector: a person who refuses to serve in the armed forces or complete military service during wartime because of moral or religious reasons

content: the ideas, characters and events in a piece

contrast: the difference(s) between two things. In literature, contrast is often used to show divisions between people or ideas

denotation: the dictionary definition of a word

denouement: the final section of a story, in which the various threads of a plot are drawn together to a resolution or a final explanation

dialogue: conversation between characters

emphasis/emphatic: stressing a point in a strong or definite way

evaluate: to assess the effectiveness of something. Evaluation in literature means to consider how effectively the writer has achieved what he or she set out to achieve

fable: a short story which provides a moral lesson

foreshadow: a literary technique in which a writer hints at future events in the story

genre: in literature, genre means the type, style or category of a text. Plays, novels and poems all belong to separate genres. Texts can also be classified by genres that relate to the style of writing – for example, thrillers or romances

ideas: what a piece of work is about; what it makes us think about

imagery: a technique, sometimes referred to as 'figurative language', used to stimulate understanding of things, ideas or people through comparisons with, for example, objects, often in original and surprising ways. Popular examples are simile and metaphor

irony: a sophisticated use of double meaning in which the 'surface' meaning is undermined by its opposite, often used to criticise or to humorous effect

juxtaposition: placing things or ideas together

list: a series of items, grouped together

literary context: where the text sits in relation to literary genres or literary traditions and how the writer might have been influenced by other writers and works of literature

metaphor: a comparison in which a writer says (or implies) one thing is another thing, both sides of the comparison sharing a similar quality

minor sentence: an ungrammatical sentence – often short – used to create impact

mood: the feelings that appear to permeate or 'spread through' a piece of writing

motif: a recurring symbol

onomatopoeia: the sound of a word imitates its meaning. It creates a vivid sense of an experience

oxymoron: a fusing of opposites to create a surprising and thought-provoking effect

paradox: a seemingly impossible combination of contradictory statements that make an interesting or compelling point

pathetic fallacy: a language technique in which aspects of the natural world reflect the emotions or events occurring within the text

personification: a technique in which an inanimate object or an idea is given human qualities. Personification can often be helpful in adding emotional intensity to a description

plosive: a definite sound made by the 'explosion' of air from the lips when we say letters such as 'b' and 'p'. It creates impact at key moments

plot: the narrative/storyline composed of the main events in a text

point of view: the perspective from which a story/literary text is told. This refers to the person or character who is delivering the story

prose: this is the 'ordinary' form of written or spoken language, one in which the language has no poetic structure and flows naturally without poetic techniques such as rhythm or rhyme. In literature, prose is normally associated with novels, short stories, essays and journalism

repetition: using the same word or expression over again, in order to emphasise the meaning of these words in the mind of the reader

rhetorical question: a question asked, not because an answer is expected but for dramatic effect and to highlight a point being made

rule of three: a list of three items that builds up to a climax in the third

setting: the place, time and/or circumstances in which experiences take place

short sentence: can add dramatic impact

sibilance: the repetition of soft sounds such as 's', 'sh', 'ch' and 'th' to create a range of effects, from gentleness to a sense of threat

simile: a comparison where one thing is said to be like another thing with similar qualities. Similes often use 'like…' or 'as…as…' to make the comparison

structure: how a work is organised and put together

symbolism: the use of symbols to represent an idea or a meaning that is not literal

theme: a central idea or key concern that a writer explores in a text. A theme is a key idea that the writer wants us to think about when reading, or after reading, the text. Themes can be explored by the writer's use of features such as characterisation, plot, structure, language, etc.

tone: a feeling that the writer aims to express. Think about tone of voice. We can recognise different tones in the way people speak, such as angry, sad, serious and ironic

transferred epithet: an expression in which an adjective is transferred from the thing it actually describes to another thing. It can express a complex idea in a compressed, dramatic and original way

word choice: the words a writer selects to convey specific meaning